BRITAIN'S BATTLE TO GO MODERN: CONFRONTING ARCHITECTURAL MODERNISMS, 1900-1925

BRITAIN'S BATTLE TO GO MODERN: CONFRONTING ARCHITECTURAL MODERNISMS, 1900-1925

Steven L. Wright

The Book Guild Ltd

First published in Great Britain in 2018 by
The Book Guild Ltd
9 Priory Business Park
Wistow Road, Kibworth
Leicestershire, LE8 0RX
Freephone: 0800 999 2982
www.bookguild.co.uk
Email: info@bookguild.co.uk
Twitter: @bookguild

Typeset in Adobe Garamond Pro

Printed and bound in Great Britain by CPI Group (UK) Ltd, Croydon, CR0 4YY

ISBN 978 1912362 813

British Library Cataloguing in Publication Data.
A catalogue record for this book is available from the British Library.

To Suzanne…
for the memories of yesterday and today
and the promises of tomorrow.

"Music, poetry, painting, architecture are all able in their different way to reach the essential soul, and the coming era will see them brought together, mutually striving to the great attainment".[1]

– Rhythm 4, Spring 1912

---

1   Michael T. H. Sadler, "After Gauguin", *Rhythm 4*, Spring 1912, pp. 23-29.

Table of Contents

Acknowledgements

In researching and writing this book I have incurred professional debts that must be acknowledged. Differing portions of *Britain's Battle to Go Modern* were presented at three academic conferences over a period of seven years. While well received, colleagues offered constructive comments and suggestions in narrowing the thesis and focusing on a smaller timeframe. I remain grateful for their interest and helpfulness in making the finished product something in which to be proud. The archives and library staffs at the British Library, the National Archives, the Tate Britain, the Royal Academy of Art and the Victoria and Albert Museum performed their curatorial duties in a gracious and professional manner. I acknowledge particularly the truly professional assistance provided by Ms. Liliana Perrone, Index Specialist, Royal Institute of British Architects (RIBA). She handled my voluminous requests with aplomb and cheerfulness. I knew I would be in good hands when, after signing in and obtaining a locker, I saw Ms. Perrone at the front desk in the Reading Room. It would be a productive day. I am appreciative of Jonathan Makepeace, Imaging Services Manager, at the RIBA who assisted me in obtaining the copyright requests for the three images reproduced from the institution's superlative photograph collection. Ms. Sarah Hart, Library Assistant for *Country Life*, and Andre Gailani, Archival Manager of *Punch Limited*, provided a similar professional service in an efficient and stress-free manner. I must acknowledge also a debt from long ago: the history professors at the University of Cincinnati who, during my undergraduate and graduate school years, imbued me with a respect for history and the accompanying challenges, pitfalls and excitement of researching and writing. A personal 'thank you' to the following individuals, some of whom are no longer with us: George B. Engberg, Zane L. Miller, Roger Daniels, John K. Alexander, Otis Mitchell, Herbert Shapiro, Bruce Levine and last, but certainly not least, Gene D. Lewis, who remained interested in my intellectual and professional development long after I departed the corridors of McMicken Hall. I owe him a special debt of gratitude.

S. L. Wright
North Yorkshire
April, 2018

"The mind of the modern architect is as the basin of the sea into which all the rivers of the past ages of architectural styles run, and it will not be strange but quite natural if this comingled ocean of ideas should present ultimately a cosmopolitan expansiveness of majestic thought, as the outcome of all its agitation".[2]

– Frank Caws, Architect, 1901

2   Frank Caws, "The Past, Present and Future of British Architecture", *The Journal of the Royal Institute of British Architects,* Vol. IX, 23 November 1901, pp. 45-48. Caws was a Sunderland – based architect responsible for such renowned structures as the Elephant Tea Rooms, Corder House and Syndenham House, all located in Sunderland.

Introduction

"There is a moment in every man's life where the soul refuses to assimilate new ideas. This hour seems to approach us stealthily, on tip-toes [sic]. We do not realise that the world is rolling on, that we are no longer able to move with it. If we do not see it, we can endure it; but to see it roll, to look at the bubbles of new ideas, to feel the outbreak of your spirits, and to be left behind with open eyes, but dull and incomprehending [sic] – were it not better to be dead?"[3]

– Ramiro de Maeztu, 1913

Historians often have analyzed Britain's tortured road toward modernism by critiquing era-defining private residences and commercial structures designed and built during the twenty-year period straddling two world wars. Although slower than Europe to embrace the "new", Britain arrived eventually in the early 1930s only to have its momentum stymied by World War II. This over-simplification does not account for subtle nuances or numerous

---

3   Ramiro de Maeztu, "Expressionism", *New Age*, 27 November 1913, pp. 122-123. De Maeztu worked as a political philosopher, journalist, literary critic and later a foreign diplomat.

complexities and, at its core, the narrative fails to consider the prolific discussions and serious angst British architects and others in society had concerning modernisms earlier in the century. The issue first arose surprisingly just before new art canvases from Europe reached British shores in 1910 and continued unabated until the 1925 *Exposition des Arts Decoratifs et Industriels Modernes* in Paris became an unexpected catalyst for reflection and gradual change.

This work is a social and cultural history of how the architectural profession – a small but important segment of British society – grappled with the cultural changes brought by modernisms. This fractious and combative relationship also offers insights into why immediately after the Great War, society, whether unable or unwilling to admit a new taxonomy of reality was necessary, found difficulty accepting the permanency of modernisms. While I have consulted several works of architectural historians and historians of modernisms, this is not a technical and analytical history of modern architectural structures or a philosophical and intellectual critique of the movement.

Those who research and study Britain's battle with modernisms are indebted in some way to Nikolaus Pevsner's 1936 seminal work, *Pioneers of the Modern Movement from William Morris to Walter Gropius*. Over the next forty years it became the widely accepted interpretation. It has come under heavy criticism in the last four decades; however, it remains an important work from which subsequent histories refer, whether in support or in disagreement with its conclusions. I do not subscribe to Pevsner's thesis that Britain's flirtation or, as he described, "England's activity in the preparation of the Modern Movement came to an end immediately after [William] Morris's death".[4] I agree partially with his argument that as the movement lost momentum in Britain, Germany and France quickly assumed control and reworked and redefined key

---

4   Nikolaus Pevsner, *Pioneers of the Modern Movement from William Morris to Walter Gropius* (London: Penguin Books, 1960), p. 27.

design philosophies. As a narrative-survey of early modernisms, Pevsner focused too heavily on landmark structures and architectural progenitors, specifically Charles Rennie Mackintosh, Frank Lloyd Wright, Adolf Loos, Louis Sullivan, Peter Behrens and Walter Gropius. He willingly accepted that Britain forfeited its leadership in "shaping the new style" only to have a proliferation of modernist designs re-emerge in the late 1920s and early 1930s, due overwhelmingly to the influx of European architects escaping political unrest and ethnic persecution.[5] Unfortunately, Pevsner failed to delve into the nitty-gritty or explain, to my satisfaction, why British architects found difficulty with design modernisms earlier in the century. He seemed to imply there had been little discussion or few concerns. Pevsner never analyzed the opinions, articles or speeches of architects that contained bountiful amounts of terrible angst, genuine concern and, yes, even magniloquent hyperbole. While he identified correctly that cultural prejudice, tradition and modernisms' leveling tendency certainly may have accounted for some of Britain's early disinterest, he failed to consider two important points: the profession's desire to define and to design a style that was uniquely British and that would not be readily embraced by other nations, and the immediate and long-term legacies of the Great War.

More recent scholarship includes Elizabeth Darling's 2007 work, *Re-Forming Britain: Narratives of Modernity Before Reconstruction.* While admitting that Pevsner's interpretation was "not without foundation or validity" she believed nonetheless it offered "only a partial view of the emergence and nature of architectural modernism in Britain... " Darling wisely departed from emphasizing what she termed "actual monuments" and concentrated instead on the process began in the 1920s – a period largely ignored by historians – of how architectural modernisms assumed a prominent role in modernizing Britain with a perdurable campaign that effectively

5   Ibid, p. 175.

"exploited prevailing tendencies".[6] Darling identified three distinct phases: when it commenced and how modernists defined both themselves and the movement; secondly, how the movement "sought to effect hegemony" by developing "narratives of modernity" that promoted the cause; and thirdly, how an eager, younger generation formulated the tools and practices that were used later during reconstruction. Perhaps most importantly and contrary to many earlier works, Darling demonstrated that modernisms had become well entrenched in Britain by 1939. Its philosophies and goals had been intertwined with assisting and solving important social, urban and industrial issues, enabling it to gain support from either select government officials or those who could assert powerful influence upon policy. These connections and support proved invaluable after 1945.

My work begins at the dawn of the 20th century in order to uncover the complexities of why it took almost a quarter century for architects and society to think seriously about going modern. The epilogue makes the necessary connections with the well-trodden narrative of Britain's successful experimentation with and increased awareness of modernisms in the late 1920s and early 1930s. I have taken a decidedly granular approach to appreciate the specific concerns that a group of well-educated, professional, socially connected and culturally engaged individuals had with design modernisms. Successive generations have dismissed or ignored both their plight and opinions as overly simplistic and lacking intellectual gravitas. This unfortunate error may have been caused by viewing past events from a contemporary perspective rather than accepting the arguments and concerns as genuine for the era no matter how pedestrian they appear today. I also consider the post-Great War period as *the* "post-war era", the way those living in the 1920s would have done, and not as "between the wars", the way those living

---

6   Elizabeth Darling, *Re-Forming Britain: Narratives of Modernity Before Reconstruction* (London: Routledge, 2007), pp. 2-4.

after 1945 could do. To interpret this period and the acceptance of modernisms any other way derails the continuity of understanding modernisms' impact on a victorious but altered society recovering from the Great War. Moreover I appreciate that modernisms, to paraphrase Marshall Berman, is best interpreted as a "maelstrom" and therefore one should not dismiss what was considered modern in 1908 or 1913 because it lacks both philosophical and physical functionalism but accept what was modern in 1946 or 1953 because it does.[7] Certainly there is consensus that whatever modernisms have been, it will remain dynamic and unpredictable.

The speeches delivered at professional meetings and the ensuing comments of colleagues made afterwards provided a rich trove of vitally relevant material that amounted to far more than mere anecdotal fodder. The plethora of articles written about modernisms by architects, artists and historians as well as editors of professional architectural and design journals offered further insights into the thoughts and ideas of those who either opposed or who supported at varying levels the essence of modernisms. The institutional archives of the Royal Institute of British Architects, the Architectural Association and the Royal Academy of Art helped explain how these august institutions reacted to modernisms' perceived apostasies. All this occurred, of course, within the backdrop of what was arguably one of the most significant periods in British history.

Similar to most historical research, there was not one definitive response whether in support of or in condemnation of modernisms that remained unaffected by the passage of time and the travails of the Great War. I have identified four defined periods that illustrate the painfully slow but ever-changing responses to modernisms. The first period dates from approximately 1900-1910 – the halcyon days of Edwardian Britain – and involved reinvigorating the initiative first pronounced in 1884 to define and then to develop *the* distinctive

---

7   Marshall Berman, *All That Is Solid Melts Into Air: The Experience of Modernity* (New York: Simon & Schuster, 1982), p. 345.

British style of architecture. A decade before the Great War cultural modernisms were in the ascent, glacially transforming architecture, fine art, music, literature and science. The British architectural profession considered these changes as nothing but a temporary fad that soon would be replaced by yet another "style". It was not long before a majority of architects began feeling insecure and a bit intimidated by the movement's dynamic and revolutionary energy.

The second era began when new designs arrived from Europe, including modern art's invasion in 1910, and ended with the war declaration in August 1914. It was during this period that architects deliberately postponed earlier efforts to redefine British architecture and instead launched a defensive movement against foreign influences in architecture. The intangible phantom of the "New Spirit" had emerged as an unwelcomed and persistent intruder. Soon a contentious debate arose pitting architects who defended the principles garnered from tradition against those who embraced the emotive precepts that sought creativity but largely ignored tradition and historical frameworks. Flummoxed by such apostasy, architects tried desperately before 1914 to marginalize modernisms' influences by redirecting their focus and attention to discrediting any modern design movements emanating from the Continent, particularly the more austere and engineered designs of Germany and Austria-Hungary.

Unfamiliarity with the burgeoning modern European art scene that also had rejected mid-nineteenth century artistic standards invited similar concerns. It raised an equal number of criticisms regarding its pernicious impact on architecture. Soon both artistic disciplines became mired in the cauldron of modernisms. Many aesthetes embraced the vanguard while others accepted the change philosophically, equating it to a death struggle of the old order in the hands of the new.[8] The majority of politicians and academic

---

8   Lewis F. Richardson, "The Old and the New", *New Age*, 31 December 1908, p. 198.

elites bristled at the new believing it an unsustainable movement that dismissed tradition, disregarded history and, with its supposed link to anarchism, was decidedly dangerous to domestic tranquility. The masses cared little if at all. A subsistence lifestyle offered limited time to ponder what must have appeared incredibly trivial.

The third era occurred during the war years and lasted until the official dedication of the Cenotaph in late 1920. The war solidified the idea of modernisms' "Germanic birth", easily facilitating its wholesale rejection by many architects. The country's dismissive attitude toward pre-war modernisms quickly disappeared once war began, reforging into a verbal bulwark focused on preventing further "foreign" infiltration. What opponents had mocked and dismissed arrogantly in peacetime as "grotesque" and "childlike" suddenly became vilified as "German", providing ready-made kindling for anti-modernists. By blindly linking most cultural modernisms to Germany and Austria-Hungary, architecture and fine art soon became a patriotic bellwether. Some banter amounted to jingoistic propaganda – a logical by-product in such a febrile atmosphere – but for many, modernisms remained an invasive pestilence that needed purging.

In the midst of world chaos discussions arose almost immediately after the war declaration about the future of architecture and fine art after achieving certain victory. Two broad but conflicting views predominated. One involved ending the "cult of ugliness" in architecture by reattempting to define *the* distinctive British style and restoring the reliance on classical traditions in fine art. The opposing but more progressive faction embraced the burgeoning modern spirit, eagerly anticipating an unpredictable golden age for both artistic disciplines.

The fourth and final era dates from late 1920 and ends in 1925 when the effort for a nostalgic return to a pre-1914 cultural reality became unrealizable and the British experience at the Paris *Exposition des Arts Decoratifs et Industriels Modernes* became the catalyst for change. After victory many in society found delusory comfort in the past but this catharsis was short lived. The war had severed the present from the past forever and unknowingly had buttressed the forces of modernism begun earlier in the century. Although no transition in history is completely smooth, it became evident by the early 1920s that British society was developing a cultural reality that eventually would force it to accept design modernisms. The conscious desire for truth and genuineness gradually replaced the veil of cultural falsehoods that had shrouded late nineteenth- and early twentieth-century life. The conflict climaxed in 1925 when the shared embarrassment of the British pavilion and items displayed at the *Exposition des Arts Decoratifs et Industriels Modernes* in Paris propelled many architects, government bureaucrats and society in general to abandon long-held beliefs that modernisms amounted to little more than transient expressions of Continental newness and novelty. Soon thereafter the nation began its reluctant but necessary transition toward a modern reality.

Britain's troubling confrontation with modernisms and the aversive conflict that transcended war and endured into the 1920s may have been most visible in the cultural confines of architecture and fine art. This potent but much overlooked struggle concerned the interdisciplinary conflict – vocationally and intellectually – between the followers of new art and architecture and traditional art and architecture. An exceedingly important controversy, this work re-examines Britain's protracted and discomforting embrace of the modern, and elucidates why it remained so difficult, to paraphrase artist Paul Nash, to "go modern and still be British".[9]

---

9   Paul Nash, "'Going Modern' and 'Being British'", *Week-end Review*, 12 March 1932, p. 322.

1

The Architects

"My opinion is that any tendency this age may have to structural beauty inclines towards elegant simplicity and an almost total absence of ornament".[10]

– Professor George Aitchison, ca. 1885

"I will not say that the latest aberrations in design are the result of paying no heed to tradition – original sin in the artists may count for something of it – but I am sure of this: that no one quite appreciative of traditional styles of design could ever have indulged in the extravagances which

---

10   E. W. Hudson, "Fifty years of Architecture," *The Builder*, Vol. LXXXVIII, 21 January 1905, p. 67. Hudson quoted from a speech delivered by Aitchison in approximately 1885 concerning the future of British architecture. Aitchison, an expert in Greek architecture, served as RIBA president from 1896-1899 and, in 1898, was a Royal Gold Medalist. His colleagues remembered him as someone who "always had something scholarly to say". *Journal of the Royal Institute of British Architects*, Vol. XVII, pp. 581, 583, 1910.

everywhere confront us in design priding itself on its entire originality".[11]

– Lewis F. Day, Author, Industrial Designer, 1908

By 1900 British architecture had reached a critical and historical stage of development. It also faced considerable trouble. When English Classicism ceased being the architectural style of choice in the 1830s-1840s, architects became preoccupied with the spectacle of charlatan revivals.[12] Accepting that the British Museum's acquisition of the Elgin Marbles had provided the inspiration for Greek revival and the newly finished Houses of Parliament gave rise to Gothic revival, it remained an era of indecision.[13] Prior constraints seemed irrelevant as architects willingly indulged in the panoply of styles dominated by fashionable eclecticism and decorative excess. They worked hard at balancing the historically familiar with the novel by altering, repositioning or reordering architectural shapes and forms. Whether pseudo-Egyptian, pseudo-Greek, pseudo-Italian Renaissance or neo-Gothic, structures reflecting each revivalist movement dotted the countryside and populated urban areas. The Queen Anne Movement that emerged in the 1870s-1880s quelled some of the revivalist obsession – especially Victorian Gothic – and, despite architects who tried desperately to convince the public it was "Free Classic", the style proved ephemeral. It disappeared by the early 1900s.[14]

---

11   Lewis F. Day, "Originality and Tradition in Design", *The Architect & Contract Reporter*, Vol. LXXIX, 10 April 1908, pp. 241-244.

12   Jonathan Glancey, *New British Architecture* (London: Thames and Hudson, Ltd., 1990), p. 10. The Greek revivalist era already was well established by the 1820s and 1830s.

13   John B. Nellist, *British Architecture and Its Background* (London: MacMillan & Co., Ltd., 1967), pp. 238-251.

14   Mark Girouard, *Sweetness and Light: The 'Queen Anne Movement', 1860-1900* (Oxford: Oxford University Press, 1977), pp. 224-227. For a broad overview of the revivalist styles see, F. R. S. Yorke, *The Modern House* (London: The Architectural Press, 1934), p. 19.

Some historians have interpreted Queen Anne ironically as another revivalist architecture that had combined early seventeenth century English Domestic work with even earlier Dutch features replete with decorative motifs.[15] Such widespread eclecticism demonstrated that by the end of the nineteenth century the profession lacked, as one historian has written, "a universally accepted grammar of architecture".[16] Many architects argued somewhat despondently that while the large quantity and sheer cost of buildings erected during the Victorian Era guaranteed they would be remembered, they equally feared that future historians would have difficulty defining the style. "No wonder we turn to the works of old for study", lamented Scottish-born but London-based architect John M. Brydon, "since we seem, as yet, indisposed to provide or unable to produce substitutes for ourselves". Dependency on the past seemed especially irksome to an architect who regularly advocated breadth and simplicity in designs at the expense of meretricious ornament.[17] "[H]ere in this giant London", Brydon argued in 1890, "where beats the pulse of the world as it never throbbed in Athens or Rome, and we are still at sixes and sevens in the matter of the arts, ready to run after the latest vagary of 'Queen Anne' or any non-descript fashion which may be anything or nothing, most probably, the latter".[18] Some went as far to interpret the fragmentation of architectural styles as a symbol of the widespread social, industrial and political discontent that had become increasingly worrisome.[19]

---

15 Alastair Service, *Edwardian Architecture and Its Origins* (London: The Architectural Press, Limited, 1975), pp. 3-9.

16 Jonathan Glancey, *New British Architecture* (London: Thames and Hudson, Ltd., 1990), p. 10.

17 John M. Brydon Obituary, *Journal of the Royal Institute of British Architects*, Vol. VIII, No. 3, 1901, p. 381.

18 John M. Brydon, "A.D. 1890", *AA Notes*, Vol. IV, February 1890, pp. 74-77.

19 Mark Girouard, *Sweetness and Light: The 'Queen Anne Movement', 1860-1900* (Oxford: Oxford University Press, 1977), pp. 224-227. These disruptions included suffragette activism as well as general labour and coal miner unrest, all of which will be detailed later.

Bleakness and pessimism did not always dominate. Years earlier, in 1884, Professor Robert Kerr of King's College London and a founder and first president of the Architectural Association, presented a paper to the Royal Institute of British Architects titled "English Architecture Thirty Years Hence". The era of the philistine and dilettante must be vanquished, he declared, for British architecture was on the cusp of a "higher style" equivalent to a new Renaissance. In a self-fulfilling prophecy wrapped in a mood of honest arrogance and obvious self-sufficiency he asked whether history finally had bequeathed Great Britain to replace France and Italy as the leader in this new movement. The answer: a resounding "yes". Employing Victorian hyperbole with a hint of Social Darwinism, he surmised that "there may be a certain vigour of manliness reserved for the English, which, in an age of increasing manliness and increasing English influence, shall accomplish unexpected results". Kerr reasoned that because Britain had assumed leadership in so many areas, it may well be the country's natural destiny to create an architectural style that would advance Anglo-Saxon civilization and lead the world. The achievement was not only worthwhile, it seemed fated. Despite the Renaissance's much-heralded accomplishments, Kerr anticipated that with British leadership great advances for architecture and art were in the offing.[20] Britain's time had arrived.

As the new century beckoned, many in the profession reaffirmed Kerr's belief that Britain's architects were on the cusp of a third historical era of cultural change, the two earlier transitions having been from Roman to Medieval and from Medieval to Renaissance.[21] A national Renaissance soon would produce what Kerr had espoused years earlier – a solidly British style of architecture. Some likened this quest for "Britishness" to the country's burgeoning overseas empire and world economic

---

20 Robert Kerr, "English Architecture Thirty Years Hence", *The Transactions of the Royal Institute of British Architects*, Vol. 34, 1883/1884, pp. 227-228.

21 R. A. Duncan, "Style and Fashion in Architecture", *The Builder*, Vol. CXXXIX, 21 November 1930, pp. 881-882.

standing.[22] Such a colossus naturally needed an architecture reflecting its greatness. Many seemed baffled that during the most significant era in British history – from unquestioned command of the seas and widespread economic and financial prosperity to technological advancements in science, medicine and industry – an architecture embodying imperial greatness had not been developed. Despite varying opinions an unbridled excitement dominated discussions about a new architecture. The prestige of the nation simply demanded it. Intertwined with the desire to create a new architecture was the Victorians' and Edwardians' belief in a linear timeline linking history with progress. Whether slow or fast, progress moved steadily onwards and upwards. Believing in the historical continuum made it perfectly natural that while showering in self-congratulation, now was the optimum time for Britain to create its own unique brand of architecture.

What exactly would comprise the new British architecture? Those who encouraged a "new" style wanted more originality and less imitation of prior eras, particularly the obsessive reverence for precedent and historicism. Many understood that by simply copying architecture from earlier periods or being hamstrung by tradition stifled self-expression and limited creativity because so few structures embodied the aspirations of the day. By abnegating any sense of originality the profession unfortunately had stagnated.[23] "[T]he idol set up for our worship at the present day is precedent", wrote the editors of *Architect & Contract Reporter*,

---

22 Arthur S. Flower, "Old and New English Architecture: A Retrospect and a Suggestion", *Journal of the Royal Institute of British Architects*, Vol. VIII, No. 3, 1901, pp. 417-418; Alan Powers, *Britain: Modern Architecture in History* (London: Reaktion Books, Ltd., 2007), pp. 13-14. The idea of an English Renaissance also included music. Many hoped Edward Elgar would increase the almost inaudible creativity of England's repertoire. Glenn Watkins, *Proof Through the Night: Music and the Great War* (Berkeley: University of California Press, 2003), p. 5.

23 "The Lay Figure: What is the British Movement in Domestic Architecture and Decoration?" *The Studio*, Vol. 23, 1901, p. 152.

and to that architects bow down and surrender up…
all energy of mind and all inventive power, rendering
themselves little better than mere automata which one
moved by the clockwork of precedent and rules. Vain is
it to look for originality and imagination so long as they
continue to be tabooed and prohibited… [24]

The editors lamented that this almost superstitious reverence for precedent suppressed creativity and impinged upon imagination.

In a recurring column that highlighted contemporary issues titled "The Lay Figure", the editors of the internationally praised and influential British design/arts journal *The Studio*, founded in 1893, openly criticized architects who continually used precedent. They had become enslaved not only by the intellectual labour of architects from earlier generations and unabashedly profited from it, but during most of the nineteenth century were guilty of something worse: design plagiarism. Untrammeled thought was as necessary in architecture and design as in science, commerce and literature. All forms of human endeavor and advancement would have stagnated long ago, the editors wrote, "were it not that genuine talent is invariably a pioneer".[25] To those with enquiring minds the message seemed clear: the millstone of historical precedent needed to be discarded or at least tempered if British architecture was to regain its creative edge.

William R. Lethaby, architect and Professor of Design at the Royal College of Art, understood that Britain never had regarded architecture as an art form worthy of expanded national energy or deep intellect. The profession preferred unfortunately to divert or to quarantine any innovative spirit into lifeless formulas. Lethaby lamented that the country seemed too preoccupied with running

---

24 "Precedent in Architecture", *The Architect & Contract Reporter*, Vol. LIV, 27 December 1895, p. 415.

25 "The Lay Figure", *The Studio,* Vol. 23, 1901, p. 152.

after the latest vagary or fashionable styles inevitably rooted in the past. While he acknowledged the importance and necessity of studying classical art and appreciating the perfect mastery of historical buildings, the real power and influence of the architect and his designs, Lethaby wrote,

> was to embody the old principle to the ever-new conditions, distinguishing and setting aside that which does not form part of the living thought of the time, which is the true objective of the true architect... not a mere interweaving of the shreds of past art, however clever, should be the informing purpose of design; all the rest is preliminary study... [26]

For architects to misdirect their considerable talents to construct "Early English" churches or "Grecian" town halls was tantamount to practising anti-architecture. Lethaby encouraged colleagues to embrace change and to strive for creativity. More importantly he implored them to design and to build for today, not yesterday.

Another preoccupation of progressive-leaning architects concerned decoration, especially the naturalistic curvilinear ornamentation popular in the late 1890s and early 1900s. Structural ornamentation was expensive and involved highly skilled craftsmen spending hours labouring to achieve the desired effect; however, because the finished product enhanced the owner's status and elevated their prestige amongst peers – especially during the late Victorian Era – the whole process seemed socially worthwhile. Even American poet Ezra Pound, newly arrived in London, complained that after British architects thought about form and had designed a fine structure, "[they] go gaga with ornaments".[27] To a nascent

---

26 William R. Lethaby, "Of the 'Motive' in Architectural Design", *AA Notes*, Vol. IV, No. 32, November 1889, pp. 23-25.

27 Ezra Pound, *Gaudier-Brzeska, A Memoir* (London: Marvell Press Edition, 1960), p. 101.

critic like Pound, architects should use only good ornament or no ornament at all. A number of architects unknowingly agreed with him, believing it imperative that ornamentation be integral to structure and not used as mere appliqué or applied as an afterthought. Such slavish dependency, they argued, lessened architecture to a level of "pretentious fussiness".[28] Nonetheless, an important concern remained. Ornamentation evoked history and tradition. Gables, columns, keystones, plinths and moldings represented the symbols and functions that had been used by the mistress art for centuries. How could the past possibly be ignored? Hoping the era of architectural excess was over, these architects endeavored to make the twentieth century an epoch of original creations. Questioning the orthodoxy of prior generations raised little concern amongst supporters of progressive innovation. They felt confident the new century would achieve a greater level of artistic creativity than the nineteenth because enthusiasm had replaced indifference and knowledge had supplanted ignorance.[29] In an oft-repeated theme, William R. Lethaby captured the essence of this prolonged dilemma in his 1910 address to the Royal Institute of British Architects:

> However desirable it might be to continue in old ways or revert to past types, it is, I feel, on reviewing the attempts which have been made, impossible. We have passed into a scientific age, and the old practical arts, produced instinctively, belong to an entirely different era.[30]

---

28 "Architecture and Painting", *The Architect & Contract Reporter*, Vol. LIII, 1 March 1895, p. 143. Adherents to this argument believed architecture must be practised as both a decorative art and a useful science; John Betjeman, *Ghastly Good Taste or a Depressing Story of the Rise and Fall of English Architecture*, (London: Chapman & Hall, Ltd. 1933), p. 122.

29 "Retrospect and Prospect", *The Builder*, Vol. LXXX, 5 January 1901, p. 2.

30 William R. Lethaby, "The Architecture of Adventure", *Journal of the Royal Institute of British Architects*, Vol. XVII, 18 April 1910, pp. 469-484.

Architects and the editors of several professional journals who opposed Lethaby's message of progressive change would accept none of it. Originators were analogous to agitators. They emphasized that classicism evoked authority within a framework honed over generations while tradition restrained and counteracted the ephemeral whims of style. More tradition needed to be invoked, not less. They did not reject inventiveness *per se* but feared architecture would continue to reflect the arbitrary constructions of recent decades if it did not follow precedent and adhere to sound principles. They did not consider tradition a "straitjacket" that hampered and stifled the movement toward modernism, quite the contrary. The history of architecture, they argued, was the history of tradition. The Renaissance in Italy and the Gothic revival in Britain broke with the tradition of the time but they did so only to return to an older tradition. To abandon tradition was unwise and, to their reasoning, impossible to contemplate. Serious architects could not fathom ignoring all that had come before. "[O]wing nothing to our predecessors", stated Henry Heathcote Stratham, noted author and editor of *The Builder*, "is to propose something which at all events has never before been proposed or attempted in the history of architecture".[31]

Traditionalists believed legitimate innovation occurred only when architects, as the structural poets of contemporary life, followed artistic rules. Those who discarded convention and created their own style were tantamount to charlatans who eventually would be discovered. "No matter in what style he attempts to disguise himself, his vulgarity is certain to betray him without being at all suspected by him… " wrote the editors of *The Architect & Contract Reporter*, "[because] he has no idea of what he ought to guard against".[32] Architect Arthur S. Flower, a sole-practitioner who

---

31 H. Heathcote Strathan, "The Order in Modern Architecture", *The Builder*, Vol. LXXXV, 7 November 1903, pp. 457-459. Address delivered to members of the Birmingham Architectural Association.

32 "Imitation in Architecture", *The Architect & Contract Reporter*, Vol. LIX, 11 March 1898, pp. 167-168.

had traveled extensively throughout Europe, Greece, Turkey and the Middle East, believed that the "spell of Rome" was too great for many. Change would never occur nor would there be a "new" British architecture; it was idle speculation to think otherwise. "Here and there a few chafe and struggle", he told colleagues at the Liverpool Architectural Society, "but for the most part we hug our chains complacently".[33]

A few architects acknowledged that while "originality at any price" was implausible, tradition needed to remain at the base of all newly conceived ideas. Tolerant traditionalists like Lewis F. Day, founding member of the Art Workers' Guild and industrial designer of stained glass, pottery and textiles who believed machinery would impact the type and quality of building ornaments of the future, considered progressive architects "so innocent of artistic appreciation as not to see how remote this restless doing [dabbling in originality] is from all that makes art worthy of respect". Day encouraged younger architects not to be so anxious to design and to build something new, modern or original, or conversely to be dissuaded from using what had been done earlier. If tradition fit the situation and was the best solution then follow through and complete the task.[34] Alexander Nisbet Paterson, a Scottish architect who had studied at the Ecole des Beaux Arts in Paris and began as a draftsman in the offices of Sir John James Burnet and later served as Governor of the Glasgow School of Art, also thought it important not to seek originality but to follow the assured lines of tradition.[35] By being true to oneself and "the requirements and opportunities

---

33 Arthur S. Flower, "Old and New English Architecture: A Retrospect and a Suggestion", *Journal of the Royal Institute of British Architects*, Vol. VIII, 27 July 1901, pp. 417-418. From a speech presented on 15 April 1901 to the Liverpool Architectural Society.

34 Lewis F. Day, "Originality and Tradition in Design", *The Architect & Contract Reporter*, Vol. LXXIX, 10 April 1908, pp. 241-244.

35 Alexander Nisbet Paterson Obituary, *Journal of the Royal Institute of British Architects*, Vol. LIV, 1947, p. 529.

of the day" the architect would find that future generations would see in this work "the special beauties and qualities of his period just as we today discover them in those of our predecessors".[36] Day and Paterson both feared for the profession's future if the perilous doctrines of what had become known as "modern school" prevailed among the younger generation. Architecture could ill afford to fall victim to the same artistic anarchy occurring within the European art world.

Some members of this faction went further. While tradition remained a core belief, they de-emphasized the need to create a definitive British style. Such an idea, they argued, was an illusion from the distant past. The inter-connectedness of the modern world – from the ease of travel to communication technologies – had made the quest obsolete and attempting such a task contradicted reality. Geographical distinctions were not growing but disappearing. "We may regret this", wrote *The Builder*, "we may think that the world was much more picturesque when each country had its own costume, but we are quite powerless to prevent it". The aesthetic and social isolation necessary for the development of a national architectural style simply no longer existed. As the reliance on locally sourced materials lessened, new ones such as reinforced concrete and structural steel had begun to be used widely, thereby limiting regional or national uniqueness. An English town hall, post office or country home would fit just as comfortably in Vienna, Paris, New York or St. Petersburg. Architecture, predicted the editors of *The Builder*, was on the cusp of creating a "world-style" based not on whimsical designs or a definitive creative or nationalistic style, but on the old reliable: classic tradition. "Tradition modified by new construction may open a new chapter in architectural history", they argued, "but tradition must be at the base of it".[37] Supporters

---

36 A. N. Paterson, "Tradition in Architecture: Its Function and Value", *The Architect & Contract Reporter*, Vol. LXVII, 25 April 1902, pp. 270-271.

37 "World Style in Architecture", *The Builder*, Vol. XLIII, 21 September 1907, pp. 305-306.

admitted that over time, classic tradition's inherent flexibility would enable significant alterations based on necessity and improved construction methods. They went as far as to predict that no single country – neither Britain, Germany nor France – could claim ownership of the new international style. As the name implied, it would belong to every nation.

In late 1901 professional differences became public in the debate over the design competition for a new cathedral in Liverpool. While architects found disfavor with several aspects of the Cathedral Committee's rules, the one that received the greatest vitriol concerned the requirement that the cathedral's style be Gothic. The editors of *The Architectural Review* pointed out that Committee members probably had not realised "how little they were appealing to the prevailing spirit in the art by prescribing a strict adherence to any historical style (be it Classic or Gothic), and how much talent they must exclude by limiting the competitors to Gothic". The editors viewed the situation so seriously that they published not only a petition signed by 295 leading British architects but several of their protest letters as well. John Belcher, an architect known for working sympathetically with painters, sculptors and general craftsmen, felt that forcing the competitors to follow old precedents would prevent any advancement of the art. "Architecture should be something living", he argued, "and not a dead imitation of past work, whether ancient or modern". John James Burnet, who later gained the reputation as "the most modern architect of his time", implored Committee members not to talk of style. "Do they not know that genius will produce a design which they will accept without question, though it is of no particular style, merely because it has evidence of that true spirit which no archeological correctness can stimulate?" Beresford Pite, a Professor of Architecture at the Royal College of Art and in partnership with John Belcher, hoped the Gothic design requirement was removed so that "the minds of architects [be] allowed liberty of thought, and some hopefulness may succeed our present unhappy despair at the

Committee's singular narrowness of view". Selwyn Image, Professor of Fine Arts at Oxford, argued that because the Committee laid down such a condition it demonstrated "a fundamental ignorance of what style is and of what art is".[38]

To appear fair and judicious, the journal also published five letters of architects who supported the Committee's requirements.[39] Perhaps not surprisingly, the words "liberty", "spirit" and "imitation" were used sparingly. George F. Bodley, an early pupil of Sir George Gilbert Scott who served later as the Superintendent Architect for York Minster and Peterborough and Southwark Cathedrals, thought Gothic was beautiful and the most poetical architecture for churches. "I cannot but think that Gothic architecture is despised by some because it is an art really unknown to them in all its infinite and elastic capabilities". W. Milner Fawcett, a graduate of Jesus College, Cambridge and in partnership with Thomas D. Atkinson, reiterated his affection for work completed in the Middle Ages, believing a Gothic design was "most suitable for English church work". Thomas Garner, another stand-out pupil of Sir George Gilbert Scott and author of *The Domestic Architecture of England During the Tudor Period* (1911), felt Gothic was the architectural style of "common sense". "It is English", he wrote, "and has been almost universally recognised as best suited for ecclesiastical purposes". Charles A. Nicholson, acknowledged to have been the most experienced architect of his generation in the Gothic style and who served as the Diocesan Architect for Chelmsford, Portsmouth, Wakefield and Winchester, argued that if the Committee insisted on a past style it might as well

---

38 "Liverpool Cathedral: A Protest and Petition", *The Architectural Review*, Vol. 10, November 1901, pp. 163-173.

39 Six architects agreed only to the second requirement that professional assessors monitor the design selection. Four architects objected to the competition altogether. The majority, however, objected to both requirements: the style must be Gothic and professional assessors monitor the selection process. "Liverpool Cathedral: A Protest and Petition", *The Architectural Review*, Vol. 10, November 1901, pp. 163-173.

be Gothic. "Surely it would be better to try and develop something from what has become a fairly well-understood type of design than to go back to the fifteenth century Italian, or seventeenth century English, or even tenth century Byzantine authorities as a basis for the design of our new twentieth century cathedral".[40]

Due to extensive protests the Committee altered its original requirement a bit and permitted designs of a Renaissance or classical style. For those trying to move British architecture away from historicism, it remained a hollow victory. The Committee chose Giles Gilbert Scott, a young and inexperienced architect, whose final product – fraught with numerous financial delays and World War II bombings – ironically lacked many of its original Gothic characteristics.

Despite the Liverpool Cathedral fracas, one area on which architects agreed was a shared disgust for the architectural style and interior designs of *L'Art Nouveau*. Few considered it a natural phase of design progression developed by professionals. While quite popular on the Continent, most British architects hoped the nation would reject its superficial influences.[41] Many believed its foreign decadence was so repugnant to British tastes that it would corrupt the purity of native design.[42] Others linked it to the unhealthy outgrowth of the new art movements and, if not controlled, certainly would harm architecture.[43] Some blamed architectural reformers. The incessant clamor for individuality had helped create the poisonous designs of *L'Art Nouveau*, which many decried as more harmful than the historicism disparaged by many progressives.[44] In response to a paper concerning furniture design delivered at the Royal Institute of British

---

40 Ibid.

41 J. Alfred Gotch, "Modern Furniture, Movable and Fixed", *Journal of the Royal Institute of British Architects*, Vol. X, 13 June 1903, pp. 401-411.

42 "The Cult of L'Art Nouveau", *The Architectural Review: A Magazine of Architecture and the Arts of Design*, Vol. XXII, July-December 1907, p. 8.

43 "Residential Flats in Germany", *Architecture & Contract Reporter*, Vol. LXXXII, 12 November 1909, pp. 305-306.

44 "The Intrusion of 'Art Nouveau' into Paris", *The Architectural Review*, Vol. XXVIII, July-December 1910, p. 85.

Architects by E. Guy Dawber, a founding member of the Council for the Preservation of Rural England, a fellow architect labeled the entire *L'Art Nouveau* style as "beneath contempt... It was only the result of a person who had lived entirely by himself, who was neglected by society and who, when he sat down to design furniture, dined off red herrings and absinthe".[45] While this emotional statement certainly did not represent the norm, it embodied the essence of disappointment that many architects felt about *L'Art Nouveau*.

In 1903, while traveling throughout the country visiting local architectural societies, John Belcher, president of the Royal Institute of British Architects from 1904-1906, elevated the discussion to a serious level. He reminded colleagues that their responsibility was to lead public taste, not follow it, especially regarding styles emanating from Europe. "We must resist as strongly as possible such insidious, enervating, and unwholesome forces", he argued, by encouraging "pure, simple and manly methods which belong to a healthy British tradition".[46] In his opening address as president in 1904, Belcher called *L'Art Nouveau* "a pernicious trick easily acquired and applied alike to buildings or jewelry, furniture or dress". Whether comprised of wood, iron, stone or glass, he likened the twisted curves to "the final stages of vegetable decay and animal decrepitude" which defied the traditional principles of construction and beauty. "It was", he concluded, "the art of fools suited to an age of fools". He urged colleagues not only to steer the public away from such hideous Continental designs but to redirect society's tastes toward aesthetics and design.[47]

---

45   E. Guy Dawber, "Furniture", *Journal of the Royal Institute of British Architects*, Vol. XIII, 24 February 1906, pp. 201-214. The quote belonged to Percy Macquoid who thanked Dawber for his "admirable and informative" address. p. 215.

46   John Belcher, "Leeds and Yorkshire Architectural Society", *The Builder*, Vol. LXXIV, 21 February 1903, p. 195.

47   John Belcher, "The Opening Address", *Journal of the Royal Institute of British Architects*, Vol. XII, 7 November 1904, pp. 1-10.

Even Charles Francis Voysey, the eponymous architect of country estates and leading arts and crafts adherent, decried its "mad eccentricity", labeling it "unhealthy" and "revolting".[48] He thought its cosmopolitan nature in particular explained British architects' reluctance to embrace the style. Arthur Stansfield Dixon, founder of the Birmingham Guild of Handicraft and a personal friend of William Morris, sounded a contented but premature sigh of relief in 1907 when he labeled the freakish designs of *L' Art Nouveau* as nothing but "a passing infection, of which the world is already nearly, if not completely, cured".[49] Two years later Ernest George, president of the Royal Institute of British Architects, declared *L' Art Nouveau* was in a "moribund state".[50] Over-confidence, however, left both men and many others ill-prepared for the radical and subjective interpretations that some European architects already had unleashed. To this small group of European architects *L' Art Nouveau* simply was not modern enough. Until British architects increased their receptiveness about the architecture of other countries they continued along a self-centered path that shunned any non-British design movement. If a design reflected a morsel of "freshness", "difference" or "novelty" detractors pounced on it as irrelevant and un-British.[51]

The reaction to the 1901 *L' Art Nouveau* exhibition at the Victoria and Albert Museum demonstrated the intense disgust shared by many in the British arts community. One critic wondered why the directors permitted curators to accession such "pretentious

---

48 Keiichi Tahara, *Art Nouveau Architecture* (London: Thames & Hudson, 2000), pp. 279-283. Voysey thought this explained why English artists and architects had some discomfort looking to the Continent for inspiration.

49 Arthur Stansfield Dixon, "Sources of Inspiration in Modern Art", *Journal of the Royal Institute of British Architects*, Vol. XV, No. 3, 1908, pp. 415-416. From a speech delivered at the Art Workers' Guild at Clifford's Inn Hall, 1 November 1907.

50 "Opening Address of Ernest George", *Journal of the Royal Institute of British Architects*, Vol. XVII, 1 November 1909, pp. 1-4.

51 "The Cult of *L'Art Nouveau*", *The Architectural Review: A Magazine of Architecture and the Arts of Design*, Vol. XXII, July-December 1907, p. 8.

trash" into a national museum. He thought a generation should pass before contemporary objects became part of the collection. What he found most deplorable, however, was its deleterious influence on students. "Art students are only too ready to catch up the most recent craze", he argued. "This ill-bred 'new art' is offered to them from every corner of Europe by the art reviews; and the one or two weedy ideas that run through it sow fresh crops wherever the seed falls". The critic lamented that the disease also had infected architecture in Germany and Austria-Hungary where "queer goitered styles have sprung up in which some decorative feature has swallowed constructive significance and beauty".[52] Another architect lamented that the caprice of modern design had captivated the attention of so many distinguished architects including Otto Wagner of Vienna who used not only poured concrete and aluminum as building materials, but applied linear functionalism for internal and external design.[53]

One favorable voice during the *L' Art Nouveau* scrap was published by *The Studio*. Far from being a sign of modern decadence and anarchy, the editors thought the movement was, in fact, "the revolt of intelligence against the tyranny of convention". It was not decadent nor revolutionary but simply modern – a natural artistic progression – "old art brought up to date". Art and design should not be constrained by rules but be free, untrammeled and inspired. When successful it represented the purest thoughts of man and reflected individual creativity. The editor heaped praise on the admirable works of architects and designers such as Josef Hoffmann, Josef Maria Olbrich, Peter Behrens and others who were leading the new renaissance, but there also were incompetent imitators who mistook "extravagance for originality and want of discipline for freedom". The editors thought the reason society rejected the movement's

---

52 "Pillory: L'Art Nouveau at South Kensington", *The Architectural Review: For the Artist & Craftsman*, Vol. 10, July-December 1901, pp. 104-105.

53 S. D. Adshead, "Style in Architecture", *Journal of the Royal Institute of British Architects*, Vol. XVI, 6 March 1909, pp. 304-308.

philosophy was because charlatans had given it a bad reputation. "You will generally find", the editors concluded, "that the man who talks loudest about his inspiration is the rankest imitator, and the most accomplished exponent of extravagant feebleness".[54]

Such vociferous reaction to *L' Art Nouveau* prevented the majority of architects from designing anything progressive or non-traditional. This aversion to newness, however, did not preclude a few pioneering architects from leaving the hermetically sealed room of classical tradition and designing innovative structures that certainly rivaled anything on the Continent. Although H. Bulkeley Creswell's Queenferry Factory, Chester (1901), John J. Burnet's proto-modernistic Kodak Warehouse and Offices, Kingsway, London (1909) and Hendrik P. Berlage's Holland House, Bury Street, City of London (1914), demonstrated dynamic talents, they generated limited enthusiasm within the profession to adopt similar forward-leaning designs. When compliments were forthcoming, they tended to be covertly dismissive. There were exceptions. Two structures in particular – William R. Lethaby's Eagle Insurance, Birmingham (1900) and Edgar Wood's evocative country home Upmeads, Stafford (1908) – exceeded anything else designed during the Edwardian Era. Wood's design especially should be heralded the most modern in pre-war Britain.[55]

---

54 "The Lay Figure: On *L'Art Nouveau*", *The Studio*, Vol. 31, 1904, p. 278.

55 Lethaby's design for the facade had elements of classicism but a year later an architectural historian argued that the columns were not classical but "nothing so much as stone versions of the legs of his [Lethaby's] furniture". The Birmingham building was the first modern building to have a bespoke inscription carved in the facade. Godfrey Rubens, "William Lethaby's Buildings" in Alastair Service, *Edwardian Architecture and Its Origins* (Wallop, Hampshire: The Architectural Press, Ltd., 1975), pp. 130-151. Hendrik P. Berlage's structure, Holland House, emphasized its vertical steel frame as well as a lobby richly decorated with colourful mosaics. Its location on what was then a narrow street with little natural light caused the structure to receive limited notice. The beginning of World War I also played a significant part in it being relegated to virtual obscurity. Alan Powers, *Britain: Modern Architecture in History*, p. 23.

Eagle Insurance Building, Birmingham, 1900 (© RIBA Collections)

Upmeads, Staffordshire, 1908 (© Country Life Picture Library)

The critic for *The Architectural Review* viewed Lethaby's Eagle Insurance Building as "a thoroughly common-sense building exactly suited to its purpose and expressive of its function; not with such delicate ornament as befits its character and is attainable under modern conditions, and of striking beauty and dignity". The four-story building was of Doulting stone where the windows of the second, third and fourth stories consisted of square-headed openings surrounded by moldings with wooden casement windows. Between every floor was a heavy projecting course of molded stonework where each course rested on a series of semi-octagonal pillars. Each course served uniquely as a brow to the windows below and as a balcony to those above. A light iron railing brought it together. Above the topmost windows, the projecting course served as a cornice of alternate semicircular and angular arches, and was itself surmounted by a parapet of mixed brick and stone with a molded stone coping. Such limited decoration enabled the critic to write happily that nowhere was there "to be found any suggestion of any past or dead style". Lethaby and his partner J. L. Ball had succeeded in designing something fresh. "[They] have given us an example of a building without archaeological or other affectation of any kind", wrote *The Architectural Review*, "whose character, or we might say style, arises from a frank recognition of modern conditions and requirements and a mastery of material and composition".[56]

The simplicity of Manchester architect Edgar Wood's Upmeads surprisingly did not shock colleagues who regularly described him as "nothing if not original".[57] Wood, who served as president of the Manchester Society of Architects and was a founding member of the Northern Art Workers' Guild, understood the

---

56 "The New Eagle Insurance Buildings, Colmore Row, Birmingham", *The Architectural Review*, Vol. 8, July-December 1900, pp. 50-53.

57 "Architecture at the Royal Academy-III", *The Builder*, Vol. 94, 30 May 1908, p. 629.

interrelationship between art and craft.[58] His work anticipated some of the best qualities of the modern movement by at least twenty years. Commissioned for Frederick Bostock of Lotus, a major shoe manufacturer, Upmeads' flat, reinforced concrete roof and geometric – almost cubist – design reflected Wood's predispositions toward the unique. Lawrence Weaver, who served later as the architectural editor of *Country Life*, wrote an effusive review: "Upmeads cannot fail, by its logical qualities, and… originality, to rivet the attention of everyone and the admiration of not a few".[59] The forecourt was formal with an axiality highlighting a recessed panel over the doorway placed within a concave arc of brick. The interior consisted of a central, two-storied, vaulted hall overlooked by a balcony at the first-floor level.[60] Contemporary reviewers labeled it "fortress-like", "lacking prettiness" and "unusual to the point of oddness".[61] While the building's austerity reflected Wood's devotion to "extreme simplicity and restraint", another contemporary reviewer asked why, in a climate that required as much light and heat as possible, it had small windows and such forbidding blank wall spaces.[62] Lawrence Weaver accepted that human nature usually rejected anything new and different, but the more important question was whether Upmeads, by abandoning traditional methods of design, carried with it "the seed of enduring betterment".[63] To Weaver's

58   Edgar Wood Obituary, *Journal of the Royal Institute of British Architects*, Vol. XVIII, No. 3, 1935, p. 212.

59   John Archer, "Edgar Wood and J. Henry Sellers: A Decade of Partnership and Experiment", in Alastair Service, *Edwardian Architecture and Its Origins* (Wallop, Hampshire: Architectural Press, Ltd., 1975), pp. 378-379.

60   Ibid. Alan Powers, *Britain: Modern Architecture in History*, pp. 21-24.

61   *Partnership in Style: Edgar Wood and J. Henry Sellers* (Manchester: Manchester City Art Gallery, 1975), p. 57; Lawrence Weaver, editor, *Small Country Houses of Today* (Suffolk: Antique Collectors Club, Baron Publishing, 1983), pp. 186-190; Nikolaus Pevsner, "Nine Swallows – No Summer", *The Architectural Review*, Vol. XCI, May 1942, pp. 109-112.

62   *The Builder*, Vol. 94, 6 June 1908, p. 666.

63   Lawrence Weaver, editor, *Small Country Houses of Today* (Suffolk: Antique Collectors Club, Baron Publishing, 1983), pp. 186-190.

mind it was a prescient structure, a harbinger of the future. Wood's colleagues, however, thought differently.

No other modern designs were forthcoming in the years preceding the Great War. British architects possessed numerous ability but seemed too insular and lacked long-term ambition to create modernistic designs, let alone revolutionary ones. The respect for tradition and nationalistic pride had become insurmountable obstacles. Most failed to grasp the possibility that modernism was not a temporary style but the vanguard of what essentially would become a complete break from the past.

Architect Charles Holden understood the relationship between architecture and contemporary society. He first gained notoriety in 1907-1908 with the controversial British Medical Association building located on the Strand in London replete with Jacob Epstein's nude statues depicting the ages of man. Although not an aggressive protagonist for modernisms, he embraced simplification and functionality while appreciating the profession could not ignore history or national tradition.[64] Although personally shy and unassuming, Holden lamented often to colleagues that, unlike scientists who embraced the era in which they lived and worked, architects were in "perpetual rebellion with the present". He wanted to awaken them from their "conservative slumber".[65] Buildings needed to be understood, Holden wrote, "as an entirely modern problem without precedent".[66] While aesthetics certainly played a part, for Holden the challenge was designing a building that functioned "smoothly, logically and economically".[67] Colleagues respected

64 Eitan Karol, *Charles Holden: Architect* (Lincolnshire, England: Shaun Tyas Publisher, 2007), pp. 174-175.

65 Richard Cork, *Art Beyond the Gallery In Early 20ᵗʰ Century England* (New Haven: Yale University Press, 1985), p. 11.

66 "Thoughts for the Strong", *The Architectural Review*, Vol. XVIII, July 1905, p. 27.

67 Karol, *Charles Holden: Architect*, pp. 174-175. Karol argued that Holden's view of "functionalism" originated with service and should not be associated with the movement style that became fashionable in the 1920s and 1930s.

Holden, believing that in the era of stylistic revivals, he stood alone by what he saved fellow architects from and by what he resisted. His most recognized structure – the Westminster underground station and 55 Broadway in London – was built later in the early 1920s. "For the first time", colleagues reflected, "it began to look as though 20th century England might manage after all to produce a 20th century architecture and not just a few experimental houses in the back streets of Chelsea and on the Chiltern heights". More than any other of his structures this demonstrated that "the rebel had arrived".[68] These accolades, however, would not be heard for almost two decades.

In the June 1905 issue of *The Architectural Review*, Holden submitted an ode that closely resembled a manifesto titled "If Whitman Had Been an Architect". The editor considered it a "remarkable outburst" from a man who "has brooded deeply over modern London". Although submitted anonymously, everyone in the profession automatically attributed it to Holden. He implored modern buildings to throw off their mantle of deceits, their cornices, pilasters, moldings, swags and scrolls, for behind and underneath the dignified proportions – the picturesque groupings, the arts and crafts prettiness and exaggerated techniques – lay what Holden loved. He urged the structure not to conceal itself.

> O! I see how subtly you have hid from the gaze of those who sought you after studio methods. But I know that you are not to be found by studio methods. The Academy and the Universities do not hold you in their formulas, and I see you laughingly evade the younger cult who seek to find you in craftsmanship.

Holden confessed that in the past he had ignored the structure's desire to be naked and free by covering it up. The time had come,

---

68   Charles Holden Obituary, *Journal of the Royal Institute of British Architects*, August 1960, p. 384.

Holden implored, to set the building free: "You shall be as naked as you choose".[69] Holden's clarion call, however, fell on deaf ears and failed to resonate with colleagues.

By the time this small coterie of "modern British designers" had demonstrated their creative zeal, the profession had thwarted, if not openly abandoned, its early leadership in architectural innovation. While one could debate if this aborted British movement was a pause or a prelude to dealing with the growing urban-industrial landscape, Germany and Austria-Hungary rapidly filled the vacuum having been enamored of the British Arts and Crafts Movement for several years.[70] Earlier in the new century architects from both nations including Josef Hoffmann and Peter Behrens, embraced Charles Rennie Mackintosh more fervently than British architects ever would.[71] Hoffmann also was praised for valuing true individualism, something that as a professor in Vienna he had imbued in his students while ensuring they did not mimic his personal style.[72] Mackintosh's designs resembled *L' Art Nouveau* so closely that many British architects thought that if continued it would harm the rectitude of native design. No such concerns existed on the Continent. Prior to 1914, many referred to the simple, contemporary designs of Peter Behrens as *Mackintoshismus*.[73] Another factor, however, became equally important.

From 1896-1903, architect Hermann Muthesius was assigned as attaché and technical reporter to the Imperial German Embassy, London, tasked with researching the engineering, architecture,

---

69 "If Whitman Had Been an Architect", *The Architectural Review*, Vol. XVII, June 1905, p. 258.

70 Wendy Kaplan, *The Arts & Crafts Movement in Europe and America: Design for the Modern World* (London: Thames & Hudson, Ltd., 2004), p. 66.

71 William J. R. Curtis, *Modern Architecture Since 1900* (London: Phaidon Press Limited, 1996), p. 330.

72 A. S. Levetus, "Otton Prutscher: A Young Viennese Designer of Interiors", *The Studio*, Vol. 37, 1906, pp. 33-41.

73 John Betjeman, *Ghastly Good Taste or a Depressing Story of the Rise and Fall of English Architecture* (London: Chapman & Hall, Ltd., 1933), p. 131.

technical education and applied arts of Britain. This activity was part of a pre-war program developed by Kaiser Wilhelm II that focused on enhancing German identity through its art and design schools curricula.[74] While Muthesius submitted numerous technical briefings, it was his detailed analysis of British country homes and lifestyle reflected by the Arts and Crafts Movement and its challenge to the oppressive opulence and eclectic crowdedness of Victorian designs that most interested German officials. The movement's all-encompassing design applications, from furniture and decorative arts to rooms and houses, personally intrigued Muthesius who eventually viewed it as a beneficial way of elevating German public taste.[75] Seven years later, in 1904, Muthesius completed his monumental three-volume work, *Das Englische Haus* (*The English House*); a genuine tour-de-force of British lifestyle. He praised the rural freshness of British domestic architecture, interior design and objects of art. Muthesius believed arts and crafts design unpretentious and, with its emphasis on "unadorned simplicity" and "minimum of forms", lacked any similarity to the twisted curves reflected in *L'Art Nouveau*. Some of the homes highlighted included Philip Webb's Red House at Bexley Heath, Charles Francis Voysey's Perrycroft at Malvern and Broad Leys on Lake Windermere, Baillie Scott's Blackwell House in Bowness-on-Windermere, and William R. Lethaby's Church of All Saints in Brockhampton. "There is an expansive, easy-going quality about the English way of life", Muthesius wrote. "The Englishman's existence is far more old-fashioned than modern;

---

74 William Owen Harrod, "The Vereinigte Staatsschulen fur freie und angewandte Kunst and the Mainstem of German Modernism", *Architectural History: Journal of the Society of Architectural Histories of Great Britain*, Vol. 52, 2009, pp. 233-269.

75 John V. Maciuika, *Before the Bauhaus: Architecture, Politics and the German State, 1890-1920* (New York: Columbia University Press, 2005), p. 82. For a detailed review of Muthesius's activities in Britain, see Chapter 2, "The Prussian Commerce Ministry and the Lessons of the British Arts and Crafts Movement".

in all its facets it bears the marks of a peaceful, traditional culture grounded in an old-established prosperity".[76]

He envied British domestic architecture and style, believing it reflected a level of modern civilization that, although lacking in Germany, might be attainable.[77] Once home, Muthesius detailed how the philosophies and polemics of less historicism and limited ornamentation – important components of the British model – could be incorporated into German architecture. His ideas met with entrenched resistance. The Kaiser's court architect, Ernst E. von Ihnen, thought that as an art form Arts and Crafts had drifted too far from elemental principles leaving in its wake only the most execrable of styles.[78] Muthesius soon became disenchanted. He left the contentious debate in 1907 to join forces with like-minded designers, architects and manufacturers and founded the *Deutscher Werkbund* (German Work Federation).[79] Under his leadership the *Werkbund's* output slowly reflected the new sensitiveness or "functionalism" that jettisoned misapplied historicism and gratuitous decorations so popular in Britain and the Continent.[80]

Muthesius was not alone in his praise of British Arts and Crafts. Throughout the late nineteenth century and in some cases predating Muthesius's visit, German designers had travelled to Britain to acquaint themselves with the "English Style". As

76 Hermann Muthesius, *The English House, Vol. 1* (London: Frances Lincoln Ltd., 2007), pp. xxvii, 219.

77 Maciuika, *Before the Bauhaus: Architecture, Politics and the German State, 1890-1920*, pp. 94-95.

78 Ernst E. von Ihnen, "Modern Architecture in Germany", *The Architect & Contract Reporter*, Vol. LXXVII, 31 May 1907, p. 359.

79 Peter Gay, *Art and Act on Causes in History – Manet, Gropius, Mondrian* (New York: Harper Row Publishers, 1976), pp. 111-114.

80 There were two 'revolutions' in German architectural style. The first occurred in the early 20th century that gave rise to the modern movement as a whole. Although narrower in scope, the second one was led by Walter Gropius and like-minded architects in 1918 after the Great War. Barbara Miller Lane, *Architecture and Politics in Germany, 1918-1945* (Cambridge: Harvard University Press, 1968), pp. 11-13.

mentioned earlier, the movement intrigued Josef Hoffmann so much so that he toured Britain several times to study designs. His meetings with Mackintosh propelled him and others to found the *Wiener Werkstatte*.[81] Hermann Obrist, a Swiss by birth who became active in Munich design, owed much of his embroidery ideas to C. R. Ashbee and the Guild of Handicraft. Karl Schmidt, founder of the *Dresdner Werkstatten fur Handwerkskunst* (Dresden Workshops for Handicraft Arts), spent a year in Britain studying artisan crafted work. He later commissioned architect Baillie Scott to create custom furniture for the workshops. Schmidt became so inspired by Ebenezer Howard's 1902 work, *Garden Cities of Tomorrow*, that from 1907-1914 he developed the first German Garden City, Hellerau. It included housing, schools, a theatre and an expanded craft factory.[82]

While some British architects and designers appreciated that cross-fertilization had occurred, it took years before others accepted that the *Werkbund* and modern German design, as well as Austria's *Wiener Werkstatte*, had British roots. A review of the 1901 Paris Exhibition praised the Austrian contributions, especially those of Josef Hoffmann who, the reviewer extolled, "is the very soul of the new movement, and his generous and fertile influence… is manifest everywhere". Hoffmann's work was considered rational, proportioned and well-balanced. He excelled at accentuating the original lines of construction where they emerged quietly with dignity and beauty. Austrian artists and decorators collectively not only had "forgotten the past", the reviewer emphasized, but their creations were free "from fetters and formulae – from everything". Their designs evoked an originality and a self-expression that vigorously embraced the modern style. If the artists remained free from outside influences, predicted the reviewer, they would

---

81 The *Weiner Werkstatte* was founded in 1903.
82 Wendy Kaplan, *The Arts and Crafts Movement in Europe and America: Design for the Modern World* (London: Thames & Hudson, Ltd., 2004), pp. 69-72.

succeed in establishing a "real, definite style of architecture and furniture".[83] Only then could the profession and society as a whole judge whether the movement was genuine or artificial.

Moreover, at the First International Exhibition of Modern Decorative Art in 1902 in Turin, Italy, another British reviewer marveled at the near-perfection of Austria's contributions. He lavished nothing except praise. The excellent but unusual designs were well-proportioned and suited to purpose. The colour schemes evoked simplicity and harmony. He wrote a bit self-effacingly but with a tinge of envy that some designs looked oddly familiar: "[I]t is with a quite legitimate pride we may note a kinship in the designs with much that for some years past we have been accustomed to see nearer home. In this case at least our influence has been for good".[84] Admitting that cross-fertilization had occurred proved easier for some to accept than others.

In July 1906, Otto Wagner attended the Royal Institute of British Architects' International Congress of Architects held in London. Regarded as the father of Austrian modernist architecture, Wagner's original work had been praised for possessing the distinctive characteristics of "lightness and grace".[85] Though he often had criticized the profession's continuing capitulation to historicism, he participated in several meetings at the conference, freely offering advice and giving

83   Gabriel Mourey, "Round the Exhibition. Austrian Decorative Art", *The Studio*, Vol. 21, 1901, pp. 113-123; Fernand Khnopff, "Josef Hoffmann – Architect and Decorator", *The Studio*, Vol. 22, 1901, pp. 261-266. In 1899, *The Studio*, overly impressed with the art scene in Austria, commented that the Secessionist exhibition and its newly completed building in Vienna "showed distinct promise for the future". Wilhelm Scholermann, "Modern Fine and Applied Art in Vienna", *The Studio*, Vol. 16, 1899, pp. 30-38.

84   William Scott, "The First International Exhibition of Modern Decorative Art, Turin, 1902", *Journal of the Royal Institute of British Architects*, Vol. IX, 27 September 1902, pp. 486-488.

85   "The Century of Architecture in Vienna", *The Builder*, Vol. CXXV, 30 November 1923, pp. 842-843.

recommendations.[86] One session in particular that Wagner chaired was titled "The Architect – Craftsman: How Far Should the Architect Receive the Theoretical and Practical Training of a Craftsman?" Included in the discussion were stalwart traditionalist and future president of the Royal Society of British Architects, Reginald Blomfield, and the progressive architect and professor, William R. Lethaby. Blomfield argued that architects should resist the tendency to disregard technique and structural design only to have it absorbed into the various crafts which, he felt, had turned their backs on tradition. Lethaby disagreed, stating that architects who studied and experienced a modicum of craft work including stone cutting, wood framing and brick handling would design and build more interesting and unique structures. Wagner believed time constraints limited the architect's ability to cultivate the necessary skills in painting, sculpture and other allied arts. He felt instead that craftsmen skills would be learned over the course of a career because a talented architect possessed "the innate gift of invention".[87] While no final decision was reached, the discussion revealed how the profession was transitioning technically, artistically and philosophically.

Wagner's visit corresponded ironically with the Imperial Royal Austrian Exhibition which ran from June-September at Earl's Court, London. While members of the International Congress of Architects may have visited the exhibition on their own, the Congress did not attend the event in mass. It opted instead to visit several historical English sites located in the home counties. In addition to showcasing the cottage industries of the Hapsburg Empire that included lacemaking and woodcarving, the exhibition offered patrons opportunities to enjoy Austrian food and drink within a fabricated Tyrolean village. More

---

86 Summary of Proceedings of the VII International Congress of Architects, 16-
    21 July 1906, *Journal of the Royal Institute of British Architects*, Vol. XIII, 1906,
    pp. iii-x.
87 Ibid.

importantly it provided the British public its first opportunity to view the modernist designs of the *Wiener Werkstatte* (Vienna Workshops) in a specially designed room. Founded in Vienna in 1903 by designers Josef Hoffmann and Koloman Moser, the workshop offered modernist design elegance, functionality and appropriateness to consumer-oriented products including furniture, glass, ceramics, silver and metalwork, jewelry, fashion and accessories.[88] As detailed earlier, its roots were influenced largely by the ideals expressed by the British Arts and Crafts Movement and the Jugendstil Movement from Central Europe. One architect who may have visited the exhibition commented later that the modern style was *the* fashion in Vienna mainly because designers had created such wonderfully tasteful objects "to which there are no precedents". He welcomed the time when this "modern style" would bring a level of wholesomeness to art throughout the world.[89]

In its review of the exhibition, *The Studio* acknowledged that Austrian decorative arts and design had advanced by "leaps and bounds", but thought the *Werkstatte* room was badly positioned causing many visitors either to hurry past or to miss it entirely. This logistical detraction, however, did not deter the journal from writing a favorable review.

It is not a little to the merit of these moderns that they turn their thoughts to every branch of manufacture, and no problem seems too difficult for them to solve. They are very earnest in all they attempt, no step is slurred over; they

---

88 Gabriele Fahr-Becker, *Wiener Werkstatte, 1903-1932* (London: Taschen GmbH, 2008), p. 217. I am indebted to Sabrina Rahman and her presentation at the Victoria and Albert Museum in late 2014 titled "The Shadow of 1914: British Architecture and Design, 1900-1925" for stressing the importance of the Imperial Austrian Exhibition, Earl's Court, London, 1906.

89 Laurence Harvey, "Modern Style", *Architecture & Contract Reporter,* Vol. LXXXII, 10 September 1909, pp. 170-172.

possess an infinite capacity for taking pains. Their success, therefore is not to be wondered at.[90]

The exhibition also enabled *The Studio* the opportunity to comment on the moribund state of the country's domestic architecture. The editors hoped some perceptible progress would have been made recently but confessed there had been little advancement. The "modern movement" had made practically no mark on what *The Studio* termed, "the more monumental works of exterior architecture". What was the problem? The often repeated response was the country was suffering from one of its serious bouts of "copyism". The second reason was the country had squandered its early leadership in the Arts and Crafts Movement, enabling European architects to rework British concepts to their liking and to gain the initiative. The editors admitted some Continental edifices were extravagant mistakes but designs that embraced "the simple motif of plain straight lines and quadratic forms" easily surpassed anything Britain had constructed recently. In towns and villages throughout Europe – wherever "contemporary" architecture had found favour – railway stations, hotels, shops, homes and churches designed along modern lines, the structures lacked any semblance of historicism and meretricious ornament. Lamenting that the modern movement had made little impact in Britain, *The Studio* took the country to task. It may not care for modernisms but if for no other reason then "proper national pride surely ought to impel her to arouse herself lest she be outstripped by other peoples in any serious application or development of the vital principles of art which may contribute to the benefit of humankind".[91]

The disinterest shown by British architects and designers in modernisms seems regrettably understandable. Unfortunately they

---

90   "Modern Decorative Art in Austria", *The Studio Yearbook of Decorative Art, 1907*, 1907, p. 211.

91   "Introduction with Especial Reference to Domestic Architecture", *The Studio Yearbook of Decorative Art, 1907*, 1907, pp. 1-3.

had fallen victim to parochial conceit allowing complacency to neutralize ambition and stifle creativity. While some acknowledged that a few colleagues had contributed to the early development of what became the "modern style" they either could not or did not want to advance it. By completely turning away from any semblance of innovation, British architects ceded the momentum to their European counterparts. Although modernisms amounted more to a sensibility and a mood than being a monolithic movement, the intellectual elitism that was part and parcel of empire had caused British architects to feel a heightened level of combative uncomfortableness with the future. This became increasingly difficult, if not impossible, after Europe introduced "foreign" elements into the design. Soon British architects felt they could no longer claim ownership of a style so void of "Britishness". This reaction only made the struggle worse and the stretch to rejoin more difficult, if not impossible.

2

The New Art Movements

"If ever there was a misnomer it was the term 'New Art'. Happily we realise by this time that what was new in it was not art, and what was art was not new, though abroad the fashion still flourishes like the wicked".[92]

– Lewis F. Day, Author, Industrial Designer, 1908

"We are now in the middle of a movement which… in an honest desire to break away from the commonplace, has gone to such unreasonable lengths that it has ceased to be sane".[93]

– The Studio, 1913

---

92 Lewis F. Day, "Originality and Tradition in Design", *The Architect & Contract Reporter*, Vol. LXXIX, 10 April 1908, pp. 241-244.

93 "The Lay Figure: On Art Crazes and Their Meaning", *The Studio*, Vol. 57, 1913, p. 350.

Architects had shown considerable interest for decades in fine art. In 1886, the Royal Institute of British Architects formed a Museum and Galleries Sub-committee responsible for reviewing art exhibitions displayed at national museums and private galleries and publishing reviews in the organization's monthly journal. The Art Standing Committee performed a similar function but dealt exclusively with reviewing architectural exhibitions and newly constructed houses and commercial buildings. The relationship between fine art and architecture was so close that every professional journal including *The Builder*, *The Architectural Review*, *The Architect & Contract Reporter*, *The Architect*, *The Journal of the Royal Institute of British Architects*, *The Builders' Journal and Architectural Engineer*, *The Architects' & Builders' Journal* and the Architectural Association's *AA Notes* regularly reviewed art exhibitions, analyzed historic art movements and discussed the newest trends in sculpture, stained, leaded and coloured glass creations, and mural paintings. An important exception remained: the publications exhibited little interest in the burgeoning modern movements in Europe. Unsurprisingly architects demonstrated a similar level of parochial conceit toward artistic modernisms as they did toward progressive building designs. It was almost as if the movements did not exist. The few who were aware thought the public would find the artworks so unpalatable there would be little clamouring for reviews because galleries and museums would never display the unsightly canvases.

British society's general awareness of early twentieth century art movements was woefully outdated at best and painfully ignorant at worst. The National Gallery rejecting the gift of a Degas painting in 1904 reflected the country's ambivalence toward recent artists. Even author/editor Ford Maddox Ford lamented that the national characteristic of Britain seemed to be "the complete absence of any art".[94] When Augustus John,

---

94 Ford Maddox Hueffer, *Thus to Revisit* (New York: E. P. Dutton and Company, 1921), pp. 136-137.

Britain's premier Bohemian-like, lyrical subject artist and one of the Slade School's "modern" products, returned home after a long hiatus in Paris, he seemed startled to find "certain persons of importance" perceived Impressionism as *the* new gospel, the very cusp of the modern movement.[95] In June 1910, the fact that *The Builder* described Fauvism – the movement that had achieved its greatest notoriety from 1904-1908 – as "the newest artistic movement to be chronicled" demonstrated how stale and old-fashioned Britain had become regarding fine art.[96] The journal editors casually dismissed the "newest" movement by stating that the Fauves simply had discovered and then raised to a higher power new fields for caricature "by enlisting colour, form and all a painter's resources in its service, and by exempting nothing on this earth from its operations".[97] Whether due to conceit or disinterest Britain's artistic aesthetic was outmoded and needed updating.

Those aware of new art pridefully celebrated Britain's isolation and reliance on tradition. One architect admitted that while it had developed at an alarming rate in Europe, "in this country the new art idea had never developed". He announced blissfully to colleagues, "[T]he same things were done today as were invented ten or twelve years ago, and the only development seemed to be in the work having got nearer to forms which were traditional".[98] A few years later, American Imagist poet John Gould Fletcher, who resided in London throughout most of the early 20th century, described the percolating combativeness of the times.

---

95 Charles Harrison, *English Art and Modernism 1900-1939* (Bloomington, Indiana: Indiana University Press, 1981), pp. 22-23; Michael Holroyd, *Augustus John: The New Biography* (London: Vintage, 1997), p. 259.

96 "The Newest New Art", *The Builder*, Vol. XLVIII, 4 June 1910, p. 628.

97 Ibid.

98 Lewis F. Day, "Originality and Tradition in Design", *The Architect & Contract Reporter*, Vol. LXXIX, 10 April 1908, pp. 241-244. A comment made by church architect and author, Louis Ambler, in response to Lewis F. Day's paper delivered to the Architectural Association.

In revolt against the elaborations of end-of-the century aestheticism, against the romantic movement faltering in sentimental prettiness, against the genteel tradition in decay, artists everywhere were turning back to the primitively ugly, knowing that in primitiveness alone lay strength.[99]

Britain would encounter this "revolt" soon but until then the new art movement appealed only to a select minority.

Some within the fine arts community appreciated that change was afoot. As early as 1894 *The Studio* discussed the importance of the German Secessionists. The editors found difficulty defining the movement but assured readers that it was not merely the "German equivalent of the New English Art Club". Although more akin to the Glasgow School, it was

neither absolutely devoted to plain air on the one hand nor fettered in abstract symbolism on the other... For all interested in modern art it would be hard to find a more pleasant way of spending a few hours than in studying and discussing these examples of a most interesting movement.

The editors believed a certain indescribable "vitality" had replaced all traces of superabundant Teutonic decoration seen in German Rococo and German neo-Gothic. With the burgeoning interest in cosmopolitan art, the editors decided to let history judge whether Continental trends would influence British art and design or vice-versa. Whatever the verdict, *The Studio* thought it a "distinctly hopeful sign" to view contemporary art with a spirit of individuality that reconciled precedent with experiment, concluding that while

---

99   John Gould Fletcher, *Life is My Song: The Autobiography of John Gould Fletcher* (New York: Farrar & Rinehart, 1937), p. 68.

some may yield disastrous results others could bring about great achievement.[100]

Before November 1910 elements of British society privy to the Continental design scene usually reacted negatively to innovation. In early 1903, Valentine Cameron Prinsep, Pre-Raphaelite artist and instructor at the Working Men's College, London, discussed contemporary fine art trends to a group of architects. He disliked Paris, believing it had wrecked more artists than it had made. "The English mind", Prinsep argued, "had a distinct means of expression and did not readily absorb the Latin feeling. Young men returned from Paris with dexterous manipulation of aggressive emphasis".[101] As a younger man he had assisted Dante Gabriel Rossetti in decorating the hall of the Oxford Union, so it seemed natural for him to feel a bit discouraged when contemporary artists painted images that shouted, "Look at me. See how cleverly I express myself". Many of these works, he argued, unfortunately reflected the personal predilections and unclear interpretations of the artists instead of the predictability of nature. "Slurring and want of care", Prinsep stated, "were proofs of being bored". He hoped artists would change focus and paint from the heart and without eccentricity instead of bowing to false gods. If they did, he felt confident Britain had nothing to "fear" about art in the twentieth century.[102] Prinsep seemed so assured that he did not offer advice if artists ignored his recommendations.

Britain's first encounter with paintings by artists referred to as "Impressionists" occurred in January-February 1905 when Grafton Galleries, London, opened the *Exhibition of Works by French Impressionists* curated by French art dealer, Paul Durand-Ruel. Over

100 G. W., "The Secessionists of Germany", *The Studio: An Illustrated Magazine of Fine and Applied Art,* Vol. 4, 1894, pp. 24-28.

101 "Mr. Prinsep's Addresses", *The Architect & Contract Reporter*, Vol. LXIX, 23 January 1903, pp. 69-70.

102 Valentine Cameron Prinsep, "Twentieth Century Art", *The Architect & Contract Reporter*, Vol. LXIX, 30 January 1903, pp. 85-86.

300 paintings were displayed, including works by Degas, Monet, Manet, Pissarro, Renoir, Morisot and Sisley and 10 pieces by Paul Cézanne, then largely unknown to British aficionados. Advertisements called it "exceptionally rich" and "unique of its kind in England".[103] "Only those who visited the Paris Exhibition of 1900 have had a chance of seeing many of them collected together", wrote *The Times*. "The leaders of the modern movement in French art can here be thoroughly appreciated and judged".[104] The irony of the exhibition, of course, was that while the paintings were considered new to the insular British, Impressionism already was out-of-date in France. Nonetheless, Renoir's work delighted the critic from *The Times* as did the paintings of Berthe Morisot. He considered Pissaro and Sisley "men of talent" and Monet a "genius". Manet painted masterpieces, argued the reviewer, while Degas lacked "even the elements of greatness". He saved his harshest criticism, however, for Cézanne whom he simply dismissed: "On M. Cézanne, the still life painter... we need not dwell".[105] Many other professional critics remained skeptical and either ignored Cézanne's work or woefully misunderstood their potential significance. Surprisingly even art critic and connoisseur, Roger Fry, remained indifferent to Cézanne, labeling him an insignificant Impressionist. His nonplussed attitude soon would change. Augustus John also seemed unswayed by Cézanne's canvases and surprisingly remained so the rest of his life.[106]

British criticisms were not limited to "obscure" French artists like Cézanne. In 1906, *Burlington Magazine* labeled a German and Austrian design exhibition as "perverse and preposterous". While the reviewer admitted some items reflected youth and energy, overall the works were too experimental and typical of the diseased "bogies

---

103 "Exhibitions Open During February 1905", *Burlington Magazine*, Vol. VI, November 1904, p. 34.

104 "French Art at the Grafton Galleries", *The Times*, 17 January 1905, p. 6.

105 Ibid.

106 Charles Harrison, *English Art and Modernism 1900-1939* (Bloomington, Indiana: Indiana University Press, 1981), pp. 22-23

of *L'Art Nouveau*". It seemed obvious, the reviewer concluded, that because art accurately reflected society only "a debased and decadent society" could create such "debased and decadent art".[107] Others took a more balanced and less reactionary position. The editors of *The Architect & Contract Reporter* argued that with new forms and sparse interpretation, modern German design represented a break with the past and a clear departure from precedent. "We may not care to imitate their architecture and painting," a British reviewer wrote, "[but] it is not unworthy of our consideration… "[108]

While these smaller exhibitions piqued the interests of a specialized few, the greater public's reaction to French art and Austrian and German design in subsequent years remained inconsequential. This indifference disappeared in June 1910 when the Brighton Municipal Art Galleries hosted an exhibition titled, *Modern French Artists – 10 June-31 August 1910*. The city's mayor sponsored the event for European tourists as an *entente cordiale*; a cultural interchange highlighting the Anglo-French military alliance created six years earlier. It was also the largest and most widely representative collection of modern French art ever exhibited in Britain.[109] The exhibition's final section elicited numerous criticisms. Britain had never experienced such art. While critics collectively labeled the works Neo-Impressionists, some took comic delight delineating specific styles: the Fauves, the Pointillists, the Vibrists, the Symbolists and the Intimists. The reviewer for *Burlington Magazine* cynically argued that

> the chief force of the exhibition lies in the special attention which it calls to the works of the Neo-Impressionists. This group of painters represents the most vigorous movement

---

107 Bernard Sickert, "Modern Painters in 1906", *Burlington Magazine*, Vol. IX, April-September 1906, pp. 221-224.

108 "Modern German Art", *The Architect & Contract Reporter*, Vol. LXXIX, 21 February 1908, pp. 123-24.

109 "Exhibition of Modern French Art at Brighton", *Burlington Magazine*, Vol. XVII, April-September, 1910, pp. 230-231.

of the movement towards a new development in art. Any movement must in its inception enlist the sympathy of all who realize that art only exists so long as it lives and moves. But movement in art is like progress in peoples, it is preferable to stagnation, but it does not constitute improvement; swine may be put in quite violent motion down steep places.[110]

The Brighton experience exposed a cultural nerve and portended greater reactions for future modern art exhibitions.

The wait was not long. A corresponding level of interest and shock increased exponentially in late 1910 with Roger Fry's groundbreaking and controversial exhibition, *Manet and the Post-Impressionists* – 8 November 1910-15 January 1911 – which ignited an all-encompassing discussion among architects and society that continued throughout the Great War and into the early 1920s.

When the exhibition opened Roger Fry was forty-four years old and a fairly recent convert to modernisms. He had graduated in 1888 with a first-class honours degree in Natural Sciences from King's College, Cambridge, but decided he wanted to paint so he left for Europe and studied art. While the quality of Fry's landscape paintings never ranked him above an amateur, his ability to communicate, to teach and to critique fine art enabled him to pursue a meaningful career. He taught art history at the Slade School of Fine Art, University College London, and helped establish the fine art journal, *Burlington Magazine*, in which he published numerous articles and critical reviews and later served as editor. Perhaps most importantly, Fry served as Curator of Painting at the New York Metropolitan Museum of Art from 1905-1910, a position he accepted after turning down the directorship of the National Gallery in London.[111]

---

110 Ibid.

111 Charles Harrison, *English Art and Modernism 1900-1939* (Bloomington, Indiana: Indiana University Press, 1981), pp. 51-52; Mary Ann Caws and Sarah Bird Wright, *Bloomsbury and France, Art and Friends* (New York: Oxford University Press, 2000), p. 25.

Fry experienced an epiphany regarding Paul Cézanne sometime during 1905-1906 after attending the *Exhibition of Works by French Impressionists* at the Grafton Galleries. Soon thereafter Fry anointed Cézanne "father of the modern movement". He came to regard Cézanne's canvases as the direct antithesis of Impressionism, "a rediscovery of those principles of structural design and harmony" that Fry had found earlier in primitive art forms.[112] In a lecture given in conjunction with the 1910 exhibition, Fry defined Post-Impressionism as "the discovery of the visual language of the imagination", arguing that art no longer had to resemble the way objects actually appeared.[113] Cézanne's work, Fry concluded, reflected everything that was "entirely distinct and personal".[114]

Manet and the Post-Impressionists exhibition was the first time many of the 25,000 visitors had seen works by Manet, Van Gogh, Cézanne and Picasso. The critics were harsh and unforgiving not only about the artwork but summarily pilloried the organizers as well. "[We] declare our belief that this art is itself a flagrant example of reaction", *The Times* wrote. "It professes to simplify, and to gain simplicity it throws away all that the long-developed skill of past artists has acquired and bequeathed. It begins all over again – and stops where a child would stop... [115] Another critic labeled Cézanne a "butcher", Gauguin a "*farceur*" and Van Gogh a "particularly

---

112 Roger Fry, *Vision and Design* (London: Chatto & Windus, 1920), p.8.

113 D. S. MacColl, *Confessions of a Keeper* (London: Alexander Maclehose & Co., 1931).

114 Denys Sutton, ed. *The Letters of Roger Fry, Vol. 1* (London: Chatto & Windus, 1972), p. 34.

115 *The Times*, November 7, 1910, p. 12. Those who opposed and disliked the exhibit did so not necessarily because of the "primitive" techniques and its "foreignness", but what it implied for the greater social and moral conductivity of England. Virginia Woolf, *Roger Fry: A Biography* (Oxford: Blackwell, 1995), p. 124; Peter Stansky, *On or About December 1910: Early Bloomsbury and Its Intimate World* (Cambridge, Massachusetts: Harvard University Press, 1996), p. 229.

disagreeable lunatic".[116] Robert Ross, critic for the *Morning Post* and editor of the works of Oscar Wilde, thought the day of the press-preview, 5 November 1910, an auspicious date to unveil "the existence of a wide-spread plot to destroy the whole fabric of European painting". He thought the Grafton Galleries served as an "admirable substitute for the vaults of Westminster – where the new Guido Fawkes, his colleagues and alleged predecessors, are exhibiting their gunpowder". Ross concluded his review with a highly polemical warning: if the movement spreads, as the exhibition catalogue professed, "it should be treated like the rat plague of Suffolk. The source of infection (e.g. the pictures) ought to be destroyed".[117] Many traditionalists believed the exhibition proved Max Nordau's controversial but popular theory from *Degeneration*, a hugely popular work first published in English in 1895, which blamed modernisms for the psychological decadence, loss of self-control and ruinous disease endemic throughout Western life.[118] In fact, an often ignored passage in Nordau's polemic singled out Britain in particular.

> Trade, industry and civilization were nowhere in the world so much developed as in England. Nowhere did men work so assiduously, nowhere did they live under such artificial conditions as there. Hence the state of degeneration and

---

116 Clive Bell, "Contemporary Art in England", *Burlington Magazine*, Vol. XXXI, 1917, pp. 30-37. Bell did not think this, he was quoting other unnamed critics.

117 Robert Ross, "The Post-Impressionists at the Grafton: The Twilight of the Idols," *Morning Post,* 7 November 1910, p. 3. After seeing works by Matisse, Ross understood why Kaiser Wilhelm dismissed an official from a Berlin Gallery who insisted on showing similar works.

118 Western decay was most obvious in the realism of Zola, the symbolism of Mallarme, Wagner's music, Ibsen's plays, Manet's pictures as well as rampant sexual freedom, women's fashion, drug addiction and nervous diseases. Barbara W. Tuchman, *The Proud Tower, A Portrait of the World Before the War: 1890-1914* (New York: Macmillan Publishing Company, 1966), p. 33.

exhaustion, which we observe today in all civilized countries as the result of this over-exertion [sic], must of necessity have shown itself sooner in England than elsewhere... [119]

Even the unconventional Bloomsbury author and social gadfly, Lytton Strachey, who relished shocking and upsetting society, disliked the exhibit, referring to it as an "aesthetic torturing of the human figure to achieve ideological significance". He enjoyed the vibrant colours of Matisse's works but considered Picasso "futuristic and incomprehensible" and Wyndham Lewis "execrable". Strachey found pleasure, however, listening and reading the other patrons' verbal and printed reactions. "I should be pleased with myself, if I were Matisse or Picasso – ," he wrote gleefully, "to be able, a humble Frenchman to perform by means of a canvas and a little paint, the extraordinary feat of making some dozen country gentlemen in England, every day for two months, grow purple in the face!"[120]

Professor Henry Tonks of the Slade Art School, University College London, professed he could not teach what he did not believe in, and urged students to "not risk contamination" and to refrain from attending the exhibition. He thought Post-Impressionism an "evil thing" that seduced gifted students away from proud British traditions.[121] Two of Tonks's students, C. R. W. Nevinson and Mark Gertler, both of whom would gain notoriety on the eve of the Great War, ignored their instructor's advice and viewed the exhibit but were not overly impressed, referring to it simply as "ultra-modernist".[122]

Author and journalist Arnold Bennett, using the pseudonym

---

119 Max Nordau, *Degeneration* (London: William Heinemann, 1895), p. 75. The work was so popular there were seven editions printed in only six months.

120 Michael Holroyd, *Lytton Strachey: The New Biography* (New York: Farrer, Straus & Giroux, 1994), p. 271.

121 David B. Haycock, *A Crisis of Brilliance: Five Young British Artists and the Great War* (London: Old Street Publishing, 2009), pp. 89-90.

122 Ibid, p. 90. Their transition to modernism remained in the future.

Jacob Tonson, wrote a scathing article in *New Age* that mocked the complacency of those who had ridiculed the paintings.

> The exhibition of the so-called 'Neo-Impressionists' over which the culture of London is now laughing, has an interest which is perhaps not confined to the art of painting. For me, personally, it has a slight, vague repercussion upon literature. The attitude of the culture of London towards it is of course merely humiliating to any Englishman who has made an effort to cure himself of insularity. It is one proof that the negligent disdain of Continental artists for English artistic opinion is fairly well founded. The mild tragedy of the thing is that London is infinitely too self-complacent even to suspect that it is London and not the exhibition which is making itself ridiculous... London may be unaware that the value of the best work of this school is permanently and definitely settled – outside London. So much the worse for London. For the movement has not only got past the guffawing stage; it has got past the arguing stage. Its authenticity is admitted by all those who have kept themselves fully awake. And in twenty years London will be signing an apology for its guffaw. It will be writing itself down an ass.[123]

Despite Bennett's lecturing, Londoners expressed relief in early 1911 when Fry's exhibit closed. The sudden exposure to modernism had been too unsettling. The affront to social decorum had become tiresome and the ambiguity of modern art disturbed many. It seemed too irrational that an artist would create a painting where one person could interpret it so differently from another person. Instead

---

123 Jacob Tonson [Arnold Bennett], "Books and Persons", *New Age*, 8 December 1910, p. 135.

of embracing the exhibition as a lesson in broadmindedness, most who visited considered it an excuse for the artists' self-promotion.

Huntley Carter, visual art critic and international editor of the modernist journal, *New Age*, lamented the exhibition's closing and modern art's departure from Britain. His gloominess illustrated a key difference between new art followers and traditionalists: interpreting individual feelings and expressions.

> We want the hero spirit in art as in all other manifestations of modern thought and action… The Post-Impressionists had it. They were able to both feel and express great emotions greatly. But the Post-Impressionists have gone and their place is occupied by picture producers who either do not experience great emotions or have the power to express them… An air of deep gloom has settled upon Grafton Galleries.[124]

If society questioned recent events, it was in the confines of London's Royal Academy of Arts where opposing modern art emerged as its *raison d'etre*. More than any organization or personality, it controlled how the country approached fine art. Many considered it the last bastion of sanity in painting and sculpture. Academic and technical instruction, public lectures and exhibitions concentrated solely on old masters and deceased artists whose talents time had bequeathed as unquestioned. Even attempts to show works of "living artists of the British School" were vetoed routinely by the ruling Council. At no time was "modern" art displayed.[125] For more advanced and daring artists the Academy did not serve as a source of inspiration or ambitious achievement but as a stodgy remnant from the past.

---

124 Huntley Carter, "Art", *New Age*, 23 February 1911, pp. 404-405.

125 Events during the war did enable a de-facto Cubist exhibit. Attempts to show works of "living artists of the British School" were vetoed routinely by the ruling Council. Detailed review of the *Annual Reports from the Council of the Royal Academy to the General Assembly of Academicians*. Royal Academy of Art Archives, London, England.

William Blake Richmond, Academy member and professor of painting from 1894-1912, addressed the modern art problem to impressionable students in an oft repeated lecture. Mirroring the institution's ethos, he found little to admire about the new movements, comparing them to the "irresponsible whims of an uncorrected child".[126] As a classical portrait artist and stained glass/mosaics craftsman who had designed frescoes and mosaics for the ceiling of St. Paul's Cathedral in London, Richmond urged caution and a reliance on the accumulated traditions garnered over centuries.

> The latest far from being necessarily of permanent value
> may be at its best only a passing fashion, a boom of novelty
> worked up by the popular press for purposes that have no
> connection with the practice of art; while at its worst,
> it may be no more than the symptom of a disease...
> It is [for the young] to cling to their great inheritance,
> recognizing the oneness of all true art and the essential
> identity of our own aspirations, hopes, fears, changes,
> vacillations with those of which history tells us. To
> follow any other course, to seek to create a new art is but
> to court the certainty of failure. Such an attempt would be
> as fatuous as an attempt to create a new morality or an
> entirely new religion.[127]

His lectures reflected concerns held by many Edwardians: embracing modern art foreshadowed the onslaught of inevitable decline, contributing to social order decay that eventually would affect morality, tradition and political stability. Therefore it was not outlandish for architects to predict that if fine art was radicalized these destructive tendencies would demolish the

---

126 William Blake Richmond, "Individuality in Modern Art", *The Builder's Journal and Architectural Engineer*, Vol. 31, 23 March 1910, pp. 217-218.

127 William Blake Richmond Lectures, 1894-1912, Royal Academy of Art Archives, London, England, Accession #2059.

long-held principal of authority in architecture with damaging consequences. By 1910 many Edwardians were losing the optimistic outlook that had defined the first years of the twentieth century. To them the sudden quest for cultural change was the opening salvo for radical social change.

Most did not have to look far afield to either read about or experience social unrest first-hand. Disturbance and change – either by strike, public demonstration or parliamentary reform – occupied the spotlight. Labour unrest, women's suffrage, House of Lords reform, Irish Home Rule and anarchist activities had created the perfect environment for a verbal assault against modernisms' invasion of architecture and fine art. "There can be few other periods when the arts mirror so faithfully the problems of the day", wrote cultural experts Wilfrid Mellers and Rupert Hildyard. "It is almost as if the artists were consciously straining to accommodate those forces which the failure of political imagination had left beyond the social pale".[128]

In 1908 and 1909 the number of workers from the building, metal, shipbuilding, and textile trades as well as from the mining/quarrying and transportation industries directly or indirectly involved in strikes and lock-outs throughout the country totaled slightly less than 300,000 per year. The number steadily increased each passing year and became progressively more violent and riotous. In 1910 the figure increased to 531 disputes involving 515,165 workers. In 1911, 903 strikes included 961,980 workers. In 1912, while the number of strikers decreased slightly to 857, the number of workers affected increased to 1.4 million. By 1913, 1,497 strikes occurred involving 688,925 workers, about 5.6 percent of the industrial population. During the first seven months of 1914, between January and July, 937 industrial strikes occurred, permitting a government official to admit that while the

---

128 Boris Ford, editor, Wilfrid Mellers and Rupert Hildyard, authors, "The Cultural and Social Setting", *The Edwardian Age and the Inter-War Years* (Cambridge: Cambridge University Press, 1989), p. 8.

time lost to labour disputes during this abbreviated period was greater than 1913, "the majority of these outstanding differences had been settled" since the war declaration. The much sought-after general strike coordinated between coal miners, railway workers and longshoremen that had been planned for the summer was prevented only because war was declared.[129] Some historians argue the action was merely postponed until 1926 when post-war economics forced the issue.

Suffragettes also vocalized their cause and between 1903 and 1914 repeatedly made their presences known. They set fire to no less than 107 buildings and slashed several paintings in museums and galleries.[130] In 1906, they disrupted proceedings in the main lobby of the House of Commons. One year later they conducted a violent march on Westminster resulting in 15 arrests. In 1908, they planned a massive march to "Rush" Parliament but were thwarted. Particularly unsettling for Londoners were the suffragettes' well organized window-breaking campaigns along busy retail streets including the Strand and Oxford and Regent streets. Windows of government buildings also were broken including the Treasury, Privy Council and Home Office. Suffragettes hit soft targets as well when they vandalized five paintings in the National Gallery and one at the Royal Academy at Burlington House. If this activity somehow seemed inadequate they set ablaze cricket clubs, racetrack clubhouses and several resort hotels throughout the country. The only quiet time was in summer 1911 when the campaigners agreed to a truce out of respect for the coronation of the new king, George V. Propriety, it seemed, had briefly triumphed.[131]

---

129 *Report on Strikes and Lock-Outs and on Conciliation and Arbitration Boards in the United Kingdom, 1913* (London: Board of Trade, 1914), pp. ii-iv.

130 Helen Carr, *The Verse Revolutionaries: Ezra Pound, H. D. and The Imagists* (London: Jonathan Cape, 2009), p. 663.

131 For a complete review of the suffragettes cause see, Andrew Rosen, *Rise Up, Women! The Militant Campaign of the Women's Social and Political Union, 1903-1914* (London: Routledge, Kegan & Paul, 1974).

Dramatic political change also was afoot. The Parliament Act 1911 gave the House of Commons dominance over the House of Lords by removing the upper chamber's right to veto appropriations bills or bills the Commons had passed three times. While the Act removed an obstacle to effectual governing and may have been considered as democratizing, it destroyed the ideal, or as an historian has argued, the "one source of traditional English feelings of security – the belief that a disinterested, benevolent legislative body existed, raised by the good fortune of birth above party pettiness, and dedicated to directing the destinies of England and the Empire".[132] Perhaps even more polarizing, it helped fuel class divisiveness by increasing the resentment of the upper classes toward what they considered their middle-class upstarts. Few disagreed that the gap had widened and would continue to expand between the two extremes in British society.

The final event that disturbed a society in flux was the complex issue of Irish Home Rule. The debate became so fraught with emotion that soon the respective volunteer military forces raised by the Unionists on one side and the Nationalists on the other outnumbered the forces of the Crown. By the summer of 1914 many in government believed civil war certainly was possible if not eminent. The Irish Home Rule Act eventually became law in September 1914 but was suspended for the duration of the Great War. This action consequently led two years later to the outbreak of violent hostilities in Ireland that endured into the early 1920s.[133]

Whether combined or taken separately these economic, social and political issues undoubtedly created a mood of helpless anxiety. These emotive issues certainly had far greater implications than colour selection or brush stroke applications, but modernists thrived on controversy. For fine art traditionalists, modernists,

---

132 Samuel Hynes, *The Edwardian Turn of Mind* (Princeton, N.J.: Princeton University Press, 1968), pp. 352.

133 For a detailed explanation of the political machinations see, Robert Tombs, *The English and Their History* (London: Allen Lane, 2014), p. 531-533.

social reformers and agitators were of the same ilk – all seemed too eager to topple long-held beliefs and standards of decorum.

The new art floodgates opened widely in 1911 after the *Post-Impressionist* exhibition closed. For three consecutive years, Britain experienced the latest creations of Cubism, Futurism and native-born Vorticism represented by Picasso, Braque, Kandinsky, Boccioni, Severini, Wadsworth, Epstein, Lewis and others.[134] Controversy continued in November 1911 when *New Age* printed Picasso's *La Mandoline et le Pernod*, the first time any British publisher had reproduced work by the artist, promptly inciting an outcry that lasted into late December. Huntley Carter of *New Age* praised Picasso who, he thought, had demonstrated that "painting has arrived at the point when, by extreme concentration, the artist attains an abstraction which to him is the soul of the subject, though this subject be composed only of ordinary objects... It indicates, too, that painting is at the point of its greatest development. It is on the threshold of the will, and not at a halting-place of men sick with inertia".[135] James Gutherie, a casual reader of *New Age*, wrote the editor that he much admired Picasso's work and was mature enough not to be bothered by the controversy.

> I am... content to know that painting is again turning towards the expression of more than its own terms. I do not mean to say that it will aim at comforting the world as the Victorians thought it should; it will no longer imitate the resemblances of things reckoned by custom to contain sentiments; but, moved and changed, painting will in itself tend to become the substance of emotion.[136]

---

134 J. B. Bullen, editor, *Post-Impressionists in England: The Critical Reception* (London: Routledge Publishing, 1988), pp. 492-501.

135 Huntley Carter, "The Plato-Picasso Idea", *New Age*, 23 November 1911, p. 88.

136 James Gutherie, "Letters to the Editor", *New Age*, 7 December 1911, pp. 141-142.

Other readers, however, remained unconvinced. One thought Picasso "had the misfortune to upset the ink [on the canvas] and tried to dry it with his boots... "[137] Harold Fisher, another regular reader of *New Age*, expressed bewildered bafflement.

> What in the name of all that is sane is the meaning of that conglomeration of blobs and scratches presented to your unoffending readers as 'A Study by Picassco'? From every conceivable standpoint have I gazed, stared, and strained my poor eyeballs at the fascinating 'study', and not a farthingsworth of rhyme or reason have I discovered in it... I appeal to you in last resort to let me know wherein lies the newness, the remarkableness and the greatness of this weird production.[138]

Criticisms of new art remained harsh as evidenced by the reaction to Picasso; however, the outcries gradually assumed a less vitriolic tone. Whatever one's personal opinion a certainty remained: artists had turned fine art on its head – once recognizable subjects became represented by unrecognizable shapes, interchangeable forms and unnatural colours. While the human connection to a painting that was praised so much in the past remained, it had become complex and less tangible. Similar to what was occurring in architecture, the intellectual debate in fine art pitted historical convention against individual creativity. A small minority realized that, like it or not, they could not dismiss the new movements as trivial fads of fashion. Although not yet willing to find new art "appealing" or even to consider it "art" at all, they nevertheless conceded it reflected the "spirit of the age"; a curious intellectual phase of the twentieth century intent on revolutionizing accepted standards. Moreover,

---

137 Gilbert Keith Chesterton, "The Unutterable", *Daily News*, 9 December 1911, p. 6.
138 Harold Fisher, "Letters to the Editor", *New Age*, 30 November 1911, p. 119.

while many differences separated all the various artistic movements they shared one common bond: painting and sculpture could not remain the exclusive purview of the "complacent elite".[139]

The Studio took a firm position in its regular feature titled "The Lay Figure". For those harnessed to the past, the journal wrote, "the sight of anything robustly alive comes to them as an unpleasant shock. Fresh air stifles them when they are dragged for a moment out of the musty atmosphere of the tomb". Those who lived constantly in the past were the ones most inclined to forget there was a "present" at all. They become so intoxicated by the past that before long they labeled everything in their own period as offensive. Society and art in general might benefit if it ceased being dependant on the artistic achievements from the past. "Art", the editors argued, "would grow stronger instead of fading away. It would become a living thing, in touch with the life of the people, not a sort of fossil dug up by men who are always burrowing underground among the dead".[140]

By gingerly accepting the new, tolerant critics offered the public a cautionary warning. Because modernists expressed emotion using non-representational shapes, forms and tones, such untraditional methods encouraged charlatanism. Armed with little ability beyond basic draughtsmanship, some artists may have thought they were expressing emotion by using parameters afforded new art, but in actuality, all they did was conceal their amateurish inabilities. In fact, when expressing the "abnormalities" of Cubism, Futurism or other modernist art movements their emotional trough may well have been empty.[141] These same critics followed up with a kernel of thoughtful advice for the wider public to consider. Failure to grasp the artist's abstract message or intent permitted many to

---

139 "The Post-Impressionist Exhibition", *The Builder*, Vol. CIII, 11 October 1912, pp. 405-406.

140 "The Lay Figure: On Looking Backward", *The Studio*, Vol. 45, 1909, p. 349.

141 "Criticism and Art", *The Architect & Contract Reporter*, Vol. LXXXIX, 28 February 1913, pp. 207-208.

discard the work as unintelligible and incoherent. It was important to remember that for many artists their work reflected a mental interpretation of what was below the surface, rather than a visual impression or exact representation on the surface. While abstraction left many cold and confused, progressive-leaning critics encouraged the public to remain sympathetic and not dismiss something it could not easily recognize at first glance. Only a patiently receptive audience could appreciate the artist's untranslatable message. John Middleton Murry, author, essayist and editor of the literary magazine *Rhythm*, echoed this sentiment when he disavowed any pretension of understanding Picasso.

> That his later work is unsaleable confirms my conviction that Picasso is one of those spirits who have progressed beyond their age. As with Plato and Leonardo, there are some paths along which pedestrian souls cannot follow, and Picasso is impelled along one of these... They who condemn Picasso condemn him because they cannot understand what he has done in the past, and are content to assume that all that is beyond their feeble comprehension is utterly bad.[142]

This advice largely went unheeded, particularly after the opening of the *Exhibition of Works by the Italian Futurist Painters* on 1 March 1912 at the Sackville Gallery, London. The opening coincided with Filippo Tommaso (F. T.) Marinetti's second trip to the city. As the self-assured and equally self-promoting leader of the Italian Futurist movement, his first visit had occurred two years earlier in April 1910 where he spoke at the Lyceum Club with a presentation entitled *Discours futuriste aux Anglais* – a flamboyant and largely unfavorable critique of British society. He thought the British were

---

142 Ibid; John Middleton Murry, "The Art of Pablo Picasso", *New Age*, 30 November 1911, pp. 115.

victims of their own traditionalism which, he believed, took on a decidedly "medieval hue, [where] the stench of musty archives and the jangling of chains still abides". The country's almost obsession with aristocracy combined with the proclivity for always appearing chic caused the British to shun impulsiveness and anything new – especially in the fine arts.[143] Armed with an insurmountable arrogance, he remained determined to make Futurism *the* avant-garde movement of its day and the Sackville Gallery exhibition provided the perfect conduit to achieve this goal.

Just as the British were tepidly beginning to understand new art, this shocking exhibition upset a fragile balance which the ever-energetic Marinetti exacerbated further with his riotous performances. The fact that the Sackville exhibition opened the same day one million miners went on strike and militant suffragettes began breaking storefront windows in London intensified matters. Such violent activity only solidified the belief that Futurism was a cipher of the nation's wider discontent.[144]

Unsurprisingly the exhibition's catalogue caused as much controversy as the paintings, infuriating unwary viewers with its inclusion of the *Foundation and Manifesto of Futurism*, followed by a joint artist statement, *The Exhibitors to the Public*, and a brief explanation of the paintings by Umberto Boccioni, Carlo Dalmazzo Carrà, Luigi Russolo, and Gino Severini. The artists declared that they were "absolutely opposed" to the art of the Post-Impressionists, Synthetists and Cubists because "they obstinately continue to paint objects motionless, frozen, and all the static aspects of nature...

---

143 F. T. Marinetti, ed. Gunter Berghaus, *Critical Writings* (New York: Farrar, Straus and Giroux, 2006), pp. 89-93. For a detailed review of Britain's response to Futurism see, Dominika Buchowska and Steven L. Wright, "The Futurist Invasion of Great Britain, 1910-1914", in Gunter Berghaus, ed., *International Yearbook of Futurism Studies, Vol. 2*, (Berlin: Walter de Gruyter & Co., 2012), pp. 201-225.

144 Lawrence Rainey, "The Creation of the Avant-garde: F. T. Marinetti and Ezra Pound", *Modernism/Modernity*, September 1994, pp. 195-219.

We, on the contrary, with points of view pertaining essentially to the future, seek for a style of motion, a thing which has never been attempted before us". Embodying the avant-garde ethos, the artists insisted that modern painting could not exist "without the starting point of an absolutely modern sensation".[145]

The antagonistic nature of the Italian movement was designed purposely to shock and cause outrage. This radical tactic proved the best way to sow the fertile territory for Futurism's expansion. The critics remained largely unconvinced and wrote unflattering reviews, but not all 40,000 visitors to the exhibition found it unworthy.[146] Writing for *The Daily Chronicle*, Charles Lewis Hind, critic, art historian and former editor and co-founder of *The Studio*, felt confident that "England as a whole will laugh at or loathe these works". Even more discouraging to Hind was the thirty-six page catalogue of explanations. When literature had to be used to understand paintings, he argued, "it ceases to be art".[147] The *Evening News* believed Futurism had "fallen flat as a breathless pancake". The paintings resembled "the most imaginative linoleum [or] the cut-paper work of a Colony Hatch Kindergarten".[148] Paul George Konody, writing for the *Pall Mall Gazette*, thought it "simply impossible" to analyse the Futurist paintings. "The majority of them", he wrote, "strike one as the pictorial rendering of confused nightmares". While acknowledging that Britain's art world had lately endured a bevy of new movements that broke from tradition, the Futurists exceeded absurdity when they declared war upon all art from both the past and the present. While grudgingly accepting that this brand of art communicated emotions, he

145 *Exhibition of Works by the Italian Futurist Painter* (London: Sackville Gallery, 1912), p. 46.

146 Charles Harrison in *English Art and Modernism, 1900-1939* (Bloomington, Indiana: Indiana University Press, 1981), p. 86.

147 Charles Lewis Hind, "Futurist Painters. Manifestos and Works of an Italian School", *The Daily Chronicle*, 4 March 1912, p. 6.

148 *Evening News,* 2 March 1912, n.p.n.

reminded Futurists that they had forgotten an equally important tenet: "Communicating emotions can only be accounted as art if it is delivered in intelligible language".[149] Philip Burne-Jones, son of the famed Pre-Raphaelite artist Edward Burne-Jones, echoed the sentiments of many Londoners when he referred to the Futurists as nothing but "a band of maniacs… outside the pale of art altogether".[150] Many British art lovers agreed and found it difficult, if not impossible, to accept the disagreeable partisanship of the Futurists.

Roger Fry offered a surprisingly tolerant, albeit cautionary, review. He found the paintings represented more of a "psychological or scientific curiosity than a work of art". Fry hoped that the Futurist's dogma would have the capacity to grow and mature. While great design relied on emotion, he felt a more positive kind – something nearer love than hate – could enable the patron to grasp the artist's intentions more completely.[151] Socialite and author Osbert Sitwell reacted favorably – at least in hindsight. Years later, he recalled that the exhibition's "lack of sensitiveness" and "literary dynamism" had caused a sense of prophecy to pervade the whole gallery. "The twentieth century", he wrote nostalgically, "with its unparalleled disasters and catastrophes, had at last smashed and bungled its way into the realms of art".[152] Walter Sickert, well-known British painter and founder of the New English Art Club, moderately criticized the Futurist's tendency to over-explain their works. Surprisingly he took issue with critics who labelled the work immoral, judging them instead to be "austere, bracing, patriotic, nationalist, positive, anti-archaistic, anti-sentimental, anti-feminist

---

149 P. G. Konody, "The Italian Futurists: Nightmare Exhibition at the Sackville Gallery", *Pall Mall Gazette*, 1 March 1912, p. 6.

150 "Sir Philip Burne-Jones and the Futurists", *Pall Mall Gazette*, 4 March 1912, p. 8.

151 Roger Fry, "Art: The Futurists", *Nation*, 9 March 1912, pp. 946-956.

152 Osbert Sitwell, *Great Morning* (London: The Preprint Society, 1949), pp. 115-116.

[and] anti-pornocratic". He thought it would behoove Britain to pay attention to the show as the nation could learn a great deal from the movement.[153]

Eight months later Fry launched the *Second Post-Impressionist Exhibition, British, French and Russian Artists* – 5 October-31 December 1912 – at London's Grafton Galleries, comprising works of fifty-two artists from three countries. Exhibiting artists included Cézanne, Picasso, Matisse, Derain, and Vlaminck from France; Spencer, Gill, Gore, Lewis, Wadsworth, Grant, Lamb, and Bell (Vanessa) from Britain; and, as an art historian referred years later, several "unexciting" Russian artists.[154] While Britain had shed some provincialism and embraced Continental art, it unsurprisingly ignored artistic developments in Germany and Austria-Hungary. It was as if, as historian Samuel Hynes posited, Britain already had separated Europe "into good and bad, or friend and foe... "[155] This attitude became more significant as time passed, affecting both art and architecture. Despite the purposeful or accidental cultural exclusion the event proved successful and exceeded all expectations for Grafton Galleries. Attendance totaled 50,000 and, from a business/financial perspective, the gallery sold most of the affordable works.[156]

While the exhibition received a calculatingly controlled response from the public, conservatives, academicians and purists greeted it with predictable contempt. Nonetheless, the strident diatribes seemed less authoritative than they had been earlier. Surprisingly and perhaps a bit blatantly, both the public and

---

153 Walter Sickert, "The Futurist 'Devil-among-the Tailors'", *English Review*, April 1912, pp. 147-152.

154 Charles Harrison, *English Art and Modernism 1900-1939* (Bloomington, Indiana: Indiana University Press, 1981), p. 62.

155 Samuel Hynes, *The Edwardian Turn of Mind* (Princeton, New Jersey: Princeton University Press, 1968), p. 335.

156 Charles Harrison, *English Art and Modernism 1900-1939* (Bloomington, Indiana: Indiana University Press, 1981), p. 61.

many within the profession recognized the merits of the new art movements. *The Builder* acknowledged the movement could not be dismissed as lacking importance. The editors admitted they did not find it interesting as "art" but instead as "a curious intellectual phase of the human spirit" that was developing in the new century. While aspects were idealistic – all works rejected any appeal to the merely sensuous – it was generally a movement of criticism, theory and experiment and should only be regarded as such. A tepid understanding did not mean total acceptance. The editors admitted the art world, as all phases of life, was in the throes of a Renaissance but if these exhibitions reflected the churnings of an emerging new order, society needed to prepare for a disquieting future.[157]

Anthony Ludovici, social critic, fervent supporter of aristocracy and hardened devotee of Friedrich Nietzsche who believed democratization was ruining fine art, found the exhibition sufferable. Whether separate or grouped together the artists proved "the decay and dissolution of art [and] their colour was the colour of decomposed tissues and of putrefying corpses". The heyday of mediocrity would not last much longer, he predicted, and encouraged artists to profit "from the confusion and doubt" they had wrought but stop trying to convince society that their efforts were "anything more than the pot-boiler paramount".[158]

The catalog's introduction of the French group written by Fry only added to the bafflement when it exclaimed that the artists

> [do] not seek to imitate form, but to create form; not to imitate life, but to find an equivalent for life. By that I mean that they wish to make images which by the clearness of their logical structure, and by their closely-knit unity of texture, shall appeal to our disinterested and contemplative

---

157 "The Post-Impressionist Exhibit", *The Builder*, Vol. CIII, 11 October 1912, pp. 405-406.

158 Anthony M. Ludovici, "Art: The Pot-Boiler Paramount", *New Age*, 21 November 1912, pp. 66-67.

imagination with something of the same vividness as the things of actual life appeal to our practical activities. In fact, they aim not at illusion, but at reality.[159]

Clive Bell's review of the British contingent also raised eyebrows by reflecting a humble but premature arrogance. Bell, who had attended Trinity College, Cambridge and upon graduation in 1902 received a scholarship to study in Paris, was a staunch supporter of French culture, food and especially fine art.[160] As a critic, author and influential member of the Bloomsbury Group, he praised the revolutionary movement, arguing that it was exactly what Britain and the art world desperately needed. Every artist, many of whom Bell considered personal friends, had something important to say. They could not have done so with any other form. The artists did not intend to please, to shock or to flatter but to "express great emotions and to provoke them". He thought the artists succeeded because they simplified themes, omitted details and concentrated on something more important – the significance of form. And a new form permitted a new way of viewing the world. He offered an epigram to explain why new art mattered: "New wine abounded and the old bottles were found wanting". Bell thought the works gained additional credence because they were "quite independent of place or time or a particular civilisation or point of view".

Theirs is an art that stands on its own feet instead of leaning upon life; and herein it differs from traditional English art, which robbed of historical and literary interest, would cease to exist. It is just because these Englishmen have expelled or reduced to servitude those romantic and irrelevant qualities that for two centuries

159 Roger Fry, *Catalogue of the Second Post-Impressionist Exhibition* (London: Grafton Galleries, 1912), p. 3.

160 Mary Ann Caws and Sarah Bird Wright, *Bloomsbury and France, Art and Friends* (New York: Oxford University Press, 2000), pp. 73-75, 93.

have made our art the laughing-stock of Europe, that they deserve as much respect and almost as much attention as superior French artists who have had no such traditional difficulties to surmount.[161]

A reader of *New Age* offered her thoughts on the exhibition. "The vague, high-sounding, and if examined-meaningless phrases scattered throughout the introduction to the catalogue", she argued, "make up a monument of bad psychology, and fail lamentably to prove the existence of any artistic value in a display of canvases which may be fitly described as a carnival of distortion".[162] For this reader and many others it remained too much. It seemed the rallying cry of "art for art's sake" amounted to nothing but a last resort of artists for whom no other sake existed.[163] Nonetheless, where the first exhibition offered astonishment, the second effort provided intellectual enrichment for those patient enough to learn.

Writing for *The Daily Chronicle*, Charles Lewis Hind heaped praise on Matisse, believing the artist merited serious consideration. "I admit that he is a trouble", Hind wrote, "disturbances always are trouble; but troubles have a way, if you take them properly, of leading to serenity". Hind argued that where Picasso would always be an experimenter who agonized toward an unreachable goal, Matisse had arrived. "He is liberating our eyes to a new kind of beauty which, if you wait for it, will sweep from his designs like music, and which rests the heavy-laden like music".[164]

Surprisingly, *The Times* offered a more positive review than it had two years earlier especially regarding the French contribution.

161 Clive Bell, "The English Group", *Catalogue of the Second Post-Impressionist Exhibition* (London: Grafton Galleries, 1912), pp. 9-12.

162 W. A. Orton, "Present Day Criticism", *New Age*, 2 May 1912, pp. 232.

163 Jocelyn Godefroi, "Form As Applied to Art", *New Age*, 12 December 1912, p. 142.

164 Charles Lewis Hind, "Ideals of Post Impressionism", *The Daily Chronicle*, 5 October 1912, p. 6.

The reviewer thought whatever label was attached to Matisse, it could not be incompetent or wilfully perverse. Quite the contrary: his work demonstrated that he possessed "great powers" full of intensity and simplicity which "carried his art very far away from the ordinary human understanding". The critic argued that Picasso too was not a charlatan but intensely original, endeavouring "to preserve himself from imitation by the pursuit of a theory scientific rather than artistic in its origin".[165] Britain's contribution was markedly inferior to the French, the critic lamented, especially in technique. Without an underlying sense of mass and form, Post-Impressionist paintings were empty. The British works resembled colour fantasies full of nonsense. The critic believed that unless the artists improved "we shall have hundreds of nonsense pictures, mere caprices in colour with no more meaning in them than a Turkey carpet". This tendency would have to cease otherwise the movement would end, like others from the past, as "an empty decorative convention".[166]

Editor and novelist Arnold Bennett cynically recorded in his diary that an important reason for the new art exhibition's popularity was that it provided "the grossly inartistic leisured class an opportunity to feel artistically superior".[167] Writing years later, Leonard Woolf offered an equally biting appraisal not of the exhibition, where he served as secretary, but of the clientele who visited.

> Large numbers of people came to the exhibition, and nine out of ten of them either roared with laughter at the pictures or were enraged by them. The British middle class

---

165 Robert Ross (attributed), "A Post-Impressionist Exhibition: Matisse and Picasso", *The Times*, 4 October 1912, p. 9.

166 Robert Ross (attributed), "The Post Impressionists: Some French and English Work", *The Times*, 21 October 1912, p. 10.

167 J. B. Bullen, editor, *Post-Impressionists in England, The Critical Reception* (London: Routledge, 1988), p. 373. Bennett's diary entry was dated 8 October 1912.

– and, as far as that goes, the aristocracy and working class
– are incorrigibly philistine, and their taste is impeccably
bad. Anything new in the arts… particularly if it is good,
infuriates them and they condemn it as either immoral
or ridiculous or both… The whole business gave me a
lamentable view of human nature, its rank stupidity and
uncharitableness… Hardly any of them made the slightest
attempt to look at, let alone understand, the pictures, and
the same inane questions or remarks were reported to me
all day long. And every now and then some well-groomed,
red-faced gentlemen, oozing the undercut of the best beef
and the most succulent of chops, carrying his top hat and
grey suede gloves, would come up to my table and abuse the
pictures and me with the greatest rudeness.[168]

Perhaps picking-up on Bennett's comments about wealthy
socialites, the satirical magazine *Punch*, poked fun at the Post-
Impressionist movement with a humourous drawing titled
"The Tapestry Mode". It portrayed a prosperous man waving a
determined right hand emphatically refusing to purchase a Post-
Impressionist work from an upscale gallery. "Noth'n' doing'!"
exclaimed the millionaire. "Why, my maiden a'nt cud Darrn a
better picture 'n that".[169] The popularity of *Punch* coupled with
its wide readership demonstrated the seriousness – albeit cloaked
in humour – that many in society felt concerning the foreign art
movements infiltrating Britain.

Months after the second Post-Impressionist exhibition closed in

168 Leonard Woolf, *Beginning Again: An Autobiography of the Years 1911-1918*
(London: Hogarth Press, 1964), pp. 93-94. Ironically, Leonard Woolf's wife,
author Virginia Woolf, could not see all the fuss: "The Grafton, thank God,
is over; artists are an abominable race. The furious excitement of these people
over their pieces of canvas coloured green and blue, is odious". Virginia Woolf
to Violet Dickinson, 24 December 1912.

169 "The Tapestry Mode", *Punch*, Vol. CXLV, 31 December 1913, p. 55.

January 1913, the editors of *The Architect & Contract Reporter* tried to digest the momentous events that had occurred the last three years and place in context the dilemma enveloping the British art community and the architectural profession: only time would judge the longevity and success of the new art movements; newness, in whatever form, always would be looked upon negatively by those who came before.

> But as long as the world lasts there will be those who are endeavouring to find fresh paths and to develop new lines of action; Pre-Raphaelites, Impressionists, Post-Impressionists, Cubists and Futurists follow one another in a ceaseless round of endeavor for fresh achievement. Some of these new paths lead to the desert, others to fresh fields and pastures new. Those who succeeded in their endeavours for fresh achievements and whose productions have at length become admitted as orthodox, will always be disposed to look askance at those who are striking out in a new direction and will regard these later revolutionists and reformers as heterodox.[170]

Understanding the new art movements proved difficult but a gradual acceptance seemed faintly visible on the fog-laden horizon.

In summer 1913, the Allied Artists Association held its annual seasonal exhibition. Founded in 1908, the organization operated on precepts similar to the *Salon des Independents* in France by regularly offering its members jury-free exhibitions. Its main purpose was to place the artists' work directly in front of the public without first submitting it for peer review. This small but potent new art component at the Royal Albert Hall exhibition received much attention. It, too, proved historic by affording the

---

170 "Notes and Comments", *The Architect & Contract Reporter*, Vol. LXXXIX, 30 May 1913, p. 539.

public an opportunity to view works by Constantin Brancusi (*Muse Endormie*) as well as Henri Gaudier-Brzeska (*Oiseau de Feu, Wrestler,* and *Madonna*). Ironically, Gaudier-Brzeska's work seemed a bit much for Imagist poet Ezra Pound who famously argued to anyone who would listen that "modern arts had a special obligation, an advanced or avant-garde duty, to go ahead of their own age and transform it".[171] Gaudier-Brzeska's talents, however, may have been too far out front even for Pound who initially laughed and snickered while viewing the *Wrestler.*[172] Well-known British sculptor, Jacob Epstein, also premiered his seminal abstract work, *Female Figure in Flenite.*[173]

The opinion of *The Architect & Contract Reporter* differed greatly from the one espoused a few months earlier by the journal's editors. It echoed the repetitive complaint that among the "Impressionist, Post-Impressionist, Aujourdhuiste, Futurist, Cubists and Divisionist revel", there included a modicum of sane art which "carries us back to the healthy manner of late Victorian work... " Surprisingly, it failed to comment on the modern pieces on display, opting instead to wax poetically about the beloved Victorian-style artworks from the past. It saved the final salvo for the catalogue, criticizing how the exhibition had been infected or, as the reviewer emphasized, "perhaps merely affected by the spirit of Post-Impressionism titles of works being

---

171 Tom Porter, *Archispeak: An Illustrated Guide to Architectural Terms* (London: Spon Press, 2004), p. 8.

172 Richard Aldington recounts in his autobiography, *Life for Life's Sake*, when Imagist poet Ezra Pound first encountered Gaudier-Brzeska. While attending the Allied Artists exhibition with his mother-in-law, he came around to viewing the *Wrestler* and, as Aldington wrote, "began capering about and making fun of it. Suddenly a gaunt sharp-faced young man, with flaming eyes and long dank hair, rushed at him and threatened him with immediate personal violence. Ezra prudently declined the combat, and at once became a warm admirer of the young man's work". Richard Aldington, *Life for Life's Sake* (New York: The Viking Press, 1941), p. 165.

173 Frank Rutter, *Art in My Time* (London: Rich & Cowan, 1933), pp. 156-157.

heedlessly transposed leaving it to the visitor to make order out of chaos".[174]

Writing anonymously, the critic from the literary magazine *The Athenaeum* showed a cautious tolerance that reflected a fresh acceptance of new art. The newest influences on art were on display, he wrote, demonstrating what was both "undeniably stimulating" and "amusing". The intent of these "would-be primitives", he argued, was to forgo any sophisticated vision and retreat instead to the "free and unspoilt eyes of a child". The reviewer cautioned artists not to be disappointed, however, if their "esoteric symbolism" was lost on the uninitiated, causing them not to receive the recognition they might possibly merit. Nonetheless, the critic offered two prescient conclusions regarding "modernists".

> First, this revolution, if it is a real revolution, cannot be checked. Secondly, it may be the immediate herald of a new Renaissance. Vaguely we seem to see here and there tokens that the consummation is close upon us. Many of these paintings and sculptures arouse not indifference, but a curious disquiet which is difficult to analyze.[175]

Roger Fry also weighed in on the exhibition. He praised the eclectic mix of styles, describing it as "the incredible jumble of conflicting ideals and aspirations of the modern world". Next to the expressive form of a Wassily Kandinsky, he wrote, were "some dear old friends [from] childhood... long-forgotten, old-world things". And alongside the "audacious simplifications" of a Constantin Brancusi or Jacob Epstein stand the "last gasps of enthusiasm for Roman pastiches of Greek art... " Fry argued that it was only here that

---

174 "The London Salon of the Allied Artists' Association, Ltd.", *The Architect & Contract Reporter*, Vol. XC, 8 August 1913, pp. 135-136. The Victorian-style artists he commended included Eva Dell, Anne Marks, Charles Prescott, A. Starling, A. B. Cull, T. C. Bell and Elinor Dowson.

175 X, "Modernism at the Albert Hall", *The Athenaeum*, 26 July 1913, pp. 92-93.

one could "trace the expiring efforts of lost causes, and forecast the menace of creeds that are not yet formulated". He heaped praise on Brancusi, feeling his works were not empty abstractions or mere exercises in plastic design but "a real interpretation of the rhythm of life… filled with a content which has been clearly and passionately apprehended". Fry found Wyndham Lewis's *Group* "remarkable", describing its somber mood and tragic intensity as "Michelangeloesque". It was the works by Kandinsky, however, that Fry found the most provocative, especially the landscape titled *Landschaft mit zwei pappeln*. He felt Kandinsky's improvisational style succeeded because after viewing it and pondering the technique, the work seemed "more definite, more logical, and closely knit in structure, more surprisingly beautiful in their color oppositions, more exact in their equilibrium. They are pure visual music… " Fry's conclusion sounded similar to the epiphany he experienced years earlier with Cézanne. He no longer doubted that abstract art could evoke emotional responses.[176]

The November 1913 *Post-Impressionist and Futurist Exhibition* at Doré Galleries, London, sought a chronological and intellectual review of painting styles that, as the catalog emphasized, had "made some noise in the world".[177] The arbitrary categorizing of the artists' work reflected both the vagueness and extensive breadth of the exhibition: Post-Impressionists, Fauvists, Neo-Impressionists, Futurists and Intimists were represented as well as works by British modernists and avant-gardists that the public had begun to associate vaguely with Futurism.[178]

An anonymous critic praised the curator's admirable intentions, but labeled the exhibition a "ponderous jest" foisted on the public. For those who needed a hearty laugh, the gallery afforded a plethora of "repellent", "piff-paffery" and "absurd" works by ungodly

---

176 Roger Fry, "The Allied Artists", *The Nation*, 2 August 1913, pp. 676-677.
177 Bullen, editor, *Post-Impressionists in England, The Critical Reception*, p. 461.
178 Extensive elements of Futurism had seeped into works by the young British artists.

"unartists" as Cézanne, Gauguin, Picasso, Van Gogh, Delaunay, Marc, Matisse, Severini, Lewis, Wadsworth, Etchells, Nevinson and, surprisingly, Sickert. If a patron wanted to pass time and be guaranteed a good laugh, they would not be disappointed.[179] To many visitors, the artists were little more than "cranks and notoriety hunters" incapable of their own individual pursuits.[180] *The Studio* wondered whether some of the artists were not "deliberately perpetrating a big practical joke on us" but tempered its viewpoint, concluding that because of the torpidity of art, it needed this level of "craziness". "The remedy, to us who are brought into contact with it, may seem to be worse than the disease", the editor argued, "but the patient derives some benefit from it, and after the shaking up is able to go about his business again in better health and with a definite renewal of vitality".[181]

Other critics seemed unappreciative. *The Daily Telegraph's* Claude Phillips, art critic and first keeper of the Wallace Collection at Hertford House in Manchester Square, Marylebone, asserted that

of those who are, rightly or wrongly, acclaimed as the precursors of the more virulent Post-Impressionism of the moment, a fair representation has been secured. And next to them, opposite them, overflowing everywhere, elbowing out the milder and less brazen votaries of modernity are the British and foreign Cubists, the humorists of the movement, with just one Futurist to give an added zest to the piquant display.[182]

---

179 "Post-Impressionist and Futurists Exhibition", *The Architect & Contract Reporter*, Vol. XC, 12 December 1913, pp. 552-553.

180 Michael J. K. Walsh, *C. R .W. Nevinson: This Cult of Violence* (Cambridge: Lutterworth, 2008), p. 61.

181 "The Lay Figure: On Art Crazes and Their Meaning", *The Studio*, Vol. 57, 1913, p. 350.

182 Claude Phillips, "Post-Impressionists", *The Daily Telegraph*, November 1913.

After viciously criticizing the British artists individually, Phillips identified an issue that perplexed aesthetes and the public alike about the modernists' factions.

> Within the group of the British extremists, though they may present an undivided front to the common enemy, there is just at present civil war; a most terrific thwacking of shields, and splintering of swords... For not even Cubism seems to bring with it equanimity; these valiant knights of the new movement, these geometers of the brush, are as quarrelsome, as little in agreement among themselves, as were the irascible doctors.[183]

Even modernist supporters found difficulty writing anything positive about the exhibition. It was as if the balance had tipped decidedly downward toward meaningless exhaustion. The effort to be innovative had become so extreme that it brought about a renewed respect for constructive principles and moderation. Clive Bell admitted in a patronizing way that "Futurism is a negligible accident, the aim of which is to squeak 'I am advanced – I am advanced'". He dismissed the British avant-garde as mere plagiarists. Even the country's "golden boy" and budding Futurist, C. R. W. Nevinson, could not escape Bell's wrath, although he fared better than most.

> Yet Nevinson bears the Briton's burden more lightly than his fellows; probably because he is cleverer than most of them. He is clever enough to pick up someone else's style with fatal ease; is he not clever enough to diagnose the malady and discover a cure?

Bell pleaded with his countrymen "to shut themselves up for six months, and paint pictures that no-one is ever going to see. They

---

183 Ibid.

might catch themselves doing something more personal if less astonishing than what they are showing at the Doré Galleries".[184]

Equally negative was the response of Imagist poet and critic John Cournos, writing for the avant-garde-oriented magazine, *The New Freewoman*. He judged the exhibition to be "a chaos of toppling cubes", a failed experiment consisting of "a little genius and much insolence". He especially was disenchanted with the British contribution, labelling it English Cubists: "Imagine, indeed, if you can, a crowd of Royal Academicians turned loose in the pastures of new art, and you have an adequate idea of the nature of English Cubism". Cournos felt the works lacked any of the dynamic quality of which modern artists often bragged. "They have little power even to irritate you – these stupid cubes, cubes without reason and cubes without soul, cubes as tedious to the eye as the sound of dominoes at the Café Royal is to the ear".[185]

Surprisingly and without any particular reason, none of the architectural journals offered opinions or reviewed art exhibitions held in early 1914. After almost ten years of serious interest they left it to circulation newspapers to critique what many considered some of the more dramatic exhibitions in the pre-war era: *First Exhibition of Works by Members of The London Group*, *The Exhibition of the Works of the Italian Futurist Painters and Sculptors*, and *20th Century Art: A Review of Modern Movements*.

The *First Exhibition of Works by Members of The London Group* opened at the Goupil Gallery on 6 March 1914. The London Group represented a loose association of artists including Post-Impressionists, Cubists and Futurists who were determined to counteract the formalism and establishment values of the Royal Academy. To the chagrin of many modernists, it also contained artists like Spencer Gore, Charles Ginner and Harold Gilman of

---

184 Clive Bell, "Art. The New Post-Impressionist Show", *Nation*, 25 October 1913, p. 172.

185 John Cournos, "The Battle of the Cubes", *The New Freewoman*, Vol. 1, 15 November 1913, pp. 214-215.

the former Camden Town Group that painted in a representational or neo-realist style.[186] In fact, *The Times* thought The London Group had divided itself along the lines of the Walter Sickert faction and the Pablo Picasso faction. Surprisingly it did not question whether the two groups should exhibit together, which it considered good for the "unity of art", but found the disparate styles bothersome and difficult to appreciate; they simply did not meld well. "It needs a sharp effort of adaptation both for the eye and for the mind", the critic wrote, "to turn from the charming interior to Miss Ethel Sands to the *Eisteddfod* of Mr. Wyndham Lewis".[187] The abrupt transition from representational art to non-representational art within the same space proved too daunting for many spectators and only increased their uncomfortableness.

The Futurists presented another exhibit in late April 1914 at the Doré Galleries, *The Exhibition of the Works of the Italian Futurist Painters and Sculptors*. It comprised not only of eighty works by Boccioni, Balla, Carrà, Severini, Soffici and Russolo, it also afforded the budding British avant-garde – including C. R. W. Nevinson, Jacob Epstein and Edward Wadsworth – the opportunity to exhibit alongside their Italian colleagues. Since the Italian movement's first exhibition two years earlier, the Futurist label had become something of a fad, attaching itself to almost anything with modernist or experimental overtones, especially in art and design circles.[188] One critic identified the Futurists as representative of "The Confetti School of Painting".[189] In a review headlined "Futurist Puzzles", another critic judged the exhibition

---

186 Sir Claude Phillips, "Goupil Gallery. The London Group", *The Daily Telegraph*, 10 March 1914, p. 5.

187 "The Cubist Error. Exhibition of the London Group", *The Times*, 7 March 1914, p. 6.

188 William Wees, *Vorticism and the English Avant-Garde* (Toronto: Toronto University Press, 1972), p. 108.

189 Unknown author, "The Confetti School of Painting", Hyman Krietman Research Centre, Tate Britain Archives.

to be provocative, referring to it as "an orgy of colours, of lines, of plants". His review included comments overheard from patrons: "'It is like my new pyjamas' says one of them pointing his finger to a wonderful mixture of yellow, purple, and blue." He went on to note, "the most amusing victim of Futurism is an old servant hanging the last paintings on the walls. It is not very easy to find out the top and bottom part of the paintings, and the poor old man had to ask the manager about every one of them".[190] The reviewer for *The Evening News* claimed that the British public saw in Futurism nothing more than a "helter-skelter conception". It not only espoused "the cult of violence for its own sake," but as an art form, it did not represent "composition but decomposition".[191] The *Daily Express* called it "Lunacy Masquerading as Art", arguing that because so much was incomprehensible, people had persuaded themselves that it must be full of meaning and significance. "There is a premium on wild, bizarre novelty," the article emphasized, "and the pursuit of truth and beauty has been almost abandoned".[192] *The Times* cautioned the public not to confuse the Futurists with an artist like Picasso who "has proved in his early works that he is an artist; and he remains one in whatever he does, however perverse it may seem to be". Not so the Futurists. *The Times* thought they might as well paint "death-bed scenes". All the works displayed appeared "commonplace" and their abstract forms too similar to the grotesque styles of *L' Art Nouveau*. "To be tired by one kind of commonplace will not deliver you from another", the critic concluded. "A chocolate-box picture remains one, even if you cut it up into little pieces and then shuffle them".[193] Unsurprisingly

190 Unknown author, "Futurist Puzzles. Baffled Critics at the Dore Galleries", Hyman Krietman Research Centre, Tate Britain Archives.

191 Unknown author, *The Evening News*, 17 April 1914, Hyman Krietman Research Centre, Tate Britain Archives.

192 "Lunacy Masquerading as Art", *Daily Express*, 20 April 1914, n.p.n.

193 "The Commonplaceness of Futurism, Dore Gallery Exhibition", *The Times*, 9 May 1914, p. 6.

the bizarreness so endemic to Futurists had made other aspects of modern art more tolerable.

The critic for *The Daily Telegraph* praised the Futurists initially, describing them as an "ingenious and verbally eloquent Italian group of painters". He then changed course. The oddest thing about the Futurists was although they had accomplished what they had set out to do and had solved their problems painting dynamic art with grandiloquent names, they had achieved nothing that was really material. "For art begins where apparently they leave off or might logically leave off", the critic argued, "had they accomplished what they have in view… " He encouraged society to search for the microbe of the disease that was attacking both art and music. "A disease", he added, "which in some phases exhales the subsidiary and serio-comic development". He ended his tongue-in-cheek clarion call with calm: Futurism in all its varieties was no real cause for alarm.[194] At its core it provided nothing more than comic relief for troubled times.

The *20ᵗʰ Century Art: A Review of Modern Movements* opened in the East End of London at the Whitechapel Gallery and ran from 8 May-20 June 1914. Artists represented included Frederick Etchells, Wyndham Lewis, C. R. W. Nevinson, David Bomberg, Duncan Grant, Mark Gertler, Henry Lamb and Vanessa Bell. As it had done previously, *The Times* warned the public it might suffer a shock. Nonetheless, it applauded Whitechapel for doing something dramatic and challenging the Royal Academy at Burlington House where "nothing at all" was happening. The critic thought it would "make those who visit it aware that there is a new movement violently different from anything in the last century… and whether you like it or dislike it you must admit that nearly every young man of talent belongs to it". Surprisingly the reviewer did not revert to condescension. He awarded the patron a minimal level of intelligence by stating that after viewing several pieces they could

---

194 "Italian Futurists Again", *The Daily Telegraph*, 28 April 1914, p. 6.

discern for themselves "the good from the bad in it almost at a glance". He reminded readers that the goal of the artists was to make art no longer a parasite of reality. Traditionally patrons judged artwork by comparing it with reality; however, artists of the new movements wanted the viewer to look at a picture without asking whether it reminded them of something else. "If it has beauty, it is an independent beauty of its own", *The Times* wrote, "and not merely a reference to something else that is beautiful". By itself, a Cubist portrait of a man might look absurd if thought of as a real man, but the real question, emphasized the critic, was whether it was absurd as an independent creation.[195] Despite years of confrontation this basic primer offered by *The Times* remained necessary for it was important for patrons to fully understand the contention of the new art movements before they thoroughly condemned them.

Claude Phillips of *The Daily Telegraph*, while not overly impressed, seemed resigned to the inevitable.

> As we have pointed out on numerous occasions, this ultra-modern – or whatever we may choose to call it – *is* here, no longer a thing of the future, but with us, upon us. It cannot be ignored, it cannot be put down purely and simply to deliberate intention to raise smoke and throw dust in the eyes of the public.

Society, he argued, could no longer relegate modern art to mere chicanery and heightened superficiality. It was here to stay. More disturbing, however, was that British culture once again had been "infected by some strange mysterious disease". As he had urged numerous times before, society must "find the microbe and apply the remedy" that hopefully would control the movement's most outrageous aspects.

---

195 "Challenge of Whitechapel to Piccadilly. An Exhibition in the East", *The Times*, 8 May 1914, p. 4.

We cannot forcibly stop up the channels along which the art of the present and the art of the future are flowing, but we may possibly… shape their course, and strike to prevent their being still further discoloured and vitiated by the innumerable side-streams which flow into them. We must do our best to distinguish… from poisonous rubbish that knows itself to be rubbish yet strives to float with the rest, impudently bumping up against its betters.[196]

Similar to many critics of both fine art and architecture in the pre-war years, Phillips blamed foreign influences for such decidedly un-British art. He reassured readers that although the artists were British, the exhibition's catalogue neglected to say that the movements displayed at the gallery – Neo-Impressionists, Post-Impressionists, Cubists and Futurists – were all "absolutely and entirely of foreign growth".[197]

Phillips also voiced concern about the venue choice. What did residents of the Whitechapel area think of the exhibition? However sincere his intention, Phillips's opinion nonetheless exposed an elitist stance of the Edwardian Era's antagonistic class structure.

The classes of persons for which this exhibition has been brought together – for we must assure that this is for them, and not for those naturally more familiar with modern art, that this is particularly intended – are those of all other which can least bear to lose the supreme consolation that great art, healer of the cruel wounds of life inevitably make, can afford.[198]

It seemed only classical fine art would help the poor and uneducated find solace and meaning in their unfulfilled and downtrodden

---

196 Sir Claude Phillips, "Art in Whitechapel. Twentieth Century Exhibition", *The Daily Telegraph*, 12 May 1914, p. 14.

197 Ibid.

198 Ibid.

lives. Their inability to garner anything uplifting from modern art, Phillips seemed to argue, was not surprising.

These last exhibitions before the onslaught of war illuminated key stylistic differences as well as tensions and fragmentations within each new art movement. Previously patrons and critics alike frequently grouped the movements within the rubric of Post-Impressionism. For many, Futurism, Post-Impressionism, Cubism and later, Vorticism, were confusingly interchangeable.[199] Critics who cynically invented names unfortunately only increased confusion. Artists also added to the general bewilderment by loudly asserting their style was superior to another artist's style or that all other interpretations were wrong. Such boisterous and egotistical behavior kept things in a state of constant turmoil, neither creating converts nor propelling the new art movements forward. Despite these inconsistencies and contradictions, however, the exhibitions demonstrated – to those patient enough to learn – that new art was not monolithic nor was it going to suddenly disappear. Moreover, these exhibitions demonstrated that the new movements were not exclusively a dalliance for the rich and wealthy to view and to comment upon, but fine art had entered *all* levels of British society. Genuine interest in new art movements may have approached an acceptable level if war had never occurred. By the early summer of 1914, Great Britain had become quite preoccupied with its social, political, economic and cultural angsts that it was left unprepared for the diplomatic turmoil and military maneuvering unfolding on the Continent. As the country redirected its focus abroad and prepared for war, modernisms suddenly assumed an entirely different and disturbing meaning.

---

199 Vorticism was founded in May 1914.

3

The Intellectual Debate Changes

"Architecture is the parent art whence all the auxiliary arts spring. Hence sculpture and painting, born as twin brothers, acknowledge architecture as a parent entitled to govern and to guide".[200]

– P. Walton Harrison, Architect, 1911

"The strongest argument in favour of creating buildings from requirements and conditions, rather than in obedience to any preconceived style or mode of expression is that it opens the way for the appeal to our higher nature and stirs up the emotions and moral sentiments".[201]

– Charles Francis Voysey, Architect, 1912

---

200 P. Walton Harrison, "Art and Its Influence Upon Daily Life", *The Architect & Contract Reporter*, Vol. LXXXVI, pp. 11-14.

201 Charles Francis Voysey, "Patriotism in Architecture", *The Builder*, Vol. CII, 29 March 1912, pp. 352-353.

A troubling issue arose in 1910: how the perceived artistic anarchy sweeping the European art world might influence British architecture. It became *the* all-encompassing topic for discussion among professional architects and lasted until the start of the Great War. The arguments appear slightly exaggerated and overzealous today but the modern movements raised serious concerns. Many architects viewed their profession as "the mistress art" – a visual rather than a business entity, thereby subjectively associated themselves with the talents of painters and sculptors rather than with the staidness of financiers and solicitors.[202] A de-facto union among architects and artists had existed since the late nineteenth century usually centering on an ideology of social relevance.[203] Although many considered sculptors, painters and designers dependent on architecture, Edward Prioleau Warren, archeologist and architect of several university buildings in Oxford, thought these artists when "at their highest and best" were the "noble parts of architecture". Oftentimes significant new buildings would be known as much for the work done by artists as for the architectural design itself. Architects hoped the relationship would grow and encouraged closer collaboration, believing it their responsibility not only to provide meaningful opportunities for stone and plaster sculptors, painters, muralists, stone carvers, wrought iron and joinery workers, and stained and coloured glass artists, but to use their skills during the interior and exterior design phases. Each profession aspired to work in sympathy with the other, eschewing any predilection to work independently. Edward Prioleau Warren believed it vitally important for each discipline to know a great deal about the other's art.

> The painter and sculptor must study architecture and understand its necessary laws and limitations, as affecting

---

202 Richard Fellows, *Edwardian Architecture: Style and Technology* (London: Lund Humphries Publisher, Ltd., 1995), pp. 12-14.

203 Deanna Petherbridge, editor, *Art For Architecture* (London: Her Majesty's Stationery Office, Department of the Environment, 1987), pp. 7-8.

their own work. And the architect must understand the other crafts; learn their requirements, and lead up to their most effective use and dispositions, regarding them not as mere desirable decorative luxuries but as essentials in any complete and noble scheme of architecture. [204]

Acknowledging a shared dependency, however, did not lessen architects' concerns. They appreciated that because of its innate flexibility art could reflect changes in society more rapidly than architecture. Fine art celebrated individualism while architecture was a social art that required collaboration and approval from interested and disinterested governmental factions. Untethered freedom allowed artists to break loose from inherited tradition more easily, causing genuine worry that if a bevy of artists – painters and sculptors in particular – ignored tradition and history and embraced art styles that incorporated abstract shapes, lines, squares and colours the results could be disastrous for architecture. Architects had drawn aesthetic inspiration from paintings for decades, but modernisms' austerity and perceived quirkiness as well as its enthusiastic utilization of primitive art styles threatened to leave architects confused and alone. The possible rejection of traditional nineteenth-century standards of art in favor of emotionally based perceptions simply proved unfathomable for most architects.

Architects reacted almost as soon as the first new art canvases reached British shores. One architect, who kept his identity a mystery, argued – perhaps a bit melodramatically – that in some cases the attempts to limit ornamentation to "obtain breadth and restraint" had caused some modern work to reflect all the deficiencies of new art: "[It] resembles nothing on the Earth beneath the heavens, and, it may be fervently hoped, resembles nothing in the heavens

---

204 Edward Prioleau Warren, "The Union of the Arts", *AA Notes*, Vol. IV, November 1889, pp. 25-26.

above".[205] In late 1909, the editors of *The Architect & Contract Reporter* commented on the exterior detail of some residential flats in Germany. The editors thought they resembled paintings from the new art movement: "[A]lways interesting", it summarized, "if <u>not</u> perhaps what we may consider uniformly successful".[206] The journal, unfortunately, did not identify the location of the flats nor provide photographs or drawings. Quite surprisingly some professionals looked favorably toward the new art movements, believing that with an increased knowledge of art, drawing and design, a new architectural style would inevitably gain a "permanent ascendancy with the highly cultivated classes" resulting in a style of truly national character that would be appreciated by everyone; one in which all artists would find "fitting expression".[207]

Despite this modicum of support the potential impact of modernism on architecture became so contentious that the debate shifted from developing a British style of architecture first pronounced by Robert Kerr in 1884, to defending the accumulated ideas and principles garnered from many sources that had stood the test of ages – tradition and authority – against modernisms' emotive precepts of challenging authority and embracing creativity with minimal dependency on historical frameworks. The intangible phantom of the "New Spirit", or as some termed it, the "Modern Spirit", emerged as a potent and unwelcomed intrusion.[208] The word "modernism" suddenly became emotive, preoccupying the profession until the Great War. By "modernisms" I ascribe to the two-tiered meaning established by John Gold. The first tier

205 Viator, "Some Thoughts on English Architecture Today", *The Architect & Contract Reporter*, Vol. LXXXI, 11 June 1909, pp. 388-389.

206 "Residential Flats in Germany", *The Architect & Contract Reporter*, Vol. LXXXII, 12 November 1909, pp. 305-306.

207 "Some Developments in Modern Architecture", *The Architect*, Vol. XLI, 22 February 1889, p. 107. An address by architect David Thomson to the Architectural Section of the Philosophical Society of Glasgow, Scotland.

208 F. M., "Authority and the Modern Spirit", *The Architects' & Builders' Journal*, Vol. 39, 22 April 1914, pp. 276-277.

concerned the search for representative forms in various media – music, art, literature and architecture – that expressed the needs and challenges of contemporary society. The second tier comprised a radical set of attitudes – about the past, toward society, toward arts and industry, and observations about daily life.[209] On whatever level modernisms presented architects with an extremely uncomfortable situation with unexpected longevity.

With provocation in the air, progressive architects questioned what had caused the cultural and intellectual restlessness of the past decade – this lust of change. The editors of *The Builder* believed social dislocation, the overindulgence of the Victorian Era, and the "unchartered liberty of an unrestrictive age" had fueled the revolt against tradition, providing a wide opening in which to criticize the existing order. Identifying the source of the discontent did not imply acceptance. Quite the opposite. While many in society wanted protection from the unrestrained clamoring, others hinted at the impossibility of mounting an effective defence.[210]

Architects believed their profession had revolved within its own isolated orbit for several decades, but this independence began to diminish as the new century beckoned. Architecture, too, had experienced an increased level of intellectual restlessness. The unstoppable "universal movement in the air" – the *zeitgeist* – which had affected music, painting, decorative arts, literature, poetry and philosophy – was inching toward the inevitable birth of a new era.[211] It was only a matter of time before its tentacles would envelop architecture. The profession could not remain immune for "no force of scholarly predilection", the editors of *The Builder* argued, "can stop the tide of a universal tendency". The movement had begun in Germany and Austria, wrote *The Builder*, where Alfred Messel,

---

209 John R. Gold, *The Experience of Modernism, Modern Architects and the Future City, 1928-1953* (London: E & FN Spoon, 1997), p. 14.

210 "Saneness in Architecture", *The Builder*, Vol. CIII, 12 July 1912, pp. 33-34.

211 "Is There A 'New Spirit' in Architecture?", *The Builder*, Vol. CIII, 1 November 1912, pp. 495-496.

Otto Wagner and others – "architects of great scholarship and great creative gifts" – abandoned the school of tradition and embarked on "a revolutionary movement".

> The tendency is revolutionary because it aims at upsetting the standards of tradition, if not altogether its canons. It says in effect we must start afresh; we have to deal not with the problems of the past, but with the changed conditions of modern life. Much of this work is experimental, a groping in the dark; much of it is also, in our view, extremely repellent. It is no longer a matter of whirling lines, splashed with forms like the figures of musical notation, which we associate with the phase of art known as *l'art nouveau* – a phase which seems happily to have passed away... It would be premature to say that we are on the eve of the birth of a new style, but there is certainly a great and universal movement in the air which may or may not be the operation of the time spirit, but which cannot be ignored.[212]

While the notion of "inevitability" sounds odd today, architects and respectable journalists were committed to the revelation of the time spirit and frequently mentioned an "uncontrollable movement toward change". While many seemed cowed by its powerful force and formidable influences, others understood that while the *zeitgeist* could not be stopped, its innate feverishness might be controlled.

In early 1912, William Howard Seth-Smith, noted church architect and watercolourist whose works had been exhibited at London's Royal Academy, addressed colleagues at the Birmingham Architectural Association. Whether called "Modernism", "Secessionism" or "Jugendstilism", the changes occurring in architecture came from a spirit of liberty and freedom exerting itself against academic precision and the canons of tradition, what he

---

212 Ibid.

termed "the element of law and order". Seth-Smith acknowledged the movement had succeeded wonderfully well in Germany and Austria because Secessionists had tempered the spirit's innate radicalism. They had confronted modern life directly and not dredged up irrelevant issues from the historical past. Seth-Smith believed Britain could be equally original and encouraged colleagues not to fight modernisms, but to merge its innovative spirit with classical tradition. He agreed that architects should be knowledgeable about the past, but thought it important to learn more from their contemporaries. Known as an architect who progressed with the times, Seth-Smith implored colleagues not to let either Greek or Roman classicism monopolize and control architectural practice to the exclusion of styles that when handled skillfully could be "more flexible and versatile in solving the complicated problems of modern civilisation… " Modernism and the spirit of freedom, according to Seth-Smith, were the driving forces for growth and progress that encouraged architects to adopt new traditions or none at all. Tradition curbed ignorant anarchy and unbridled individuality and it was the architect's job to understand these complementary forces. "Excessive individualism means energy without order", he argued. "Excessive socialism, order without energy… It is the task of our professors to teach the true relationship of these complementary forces. Let us neither encourage the monotony of cultured mediocrity nor endure vulgar originality".[213]

The accolades Seth-Smith bestowed on Secessionist designs from Germany and Austria derived partly from his extensive travels on the Continent and the knowledge he had garnered from a series

---

213 Ibid. Seth-Smith mentioned Otto Wagner and Alfred Messel specifically. William Howard Seth-Smith, "Modernism and Authority in Architectural Design", *Journal of the Royal Institute of British Architects,* Vol. XIX, 1912, pp. 678-682; "Obituary, William Howard Seth-Smith", *Journal of the Royal Institute of British Architects,* Vol. XXXVI, 1929, p. 122; Seth-Smith served as president of the Society of Architects from 1881-1891 and as president of the Architectural Association from 1900-1902.

of articles in *Architect & Contract Reporter* from 1910-1914 titled "Modern European Architecture". The photographs highlighted newly constructed buildings, homes, storefronts and churches throughout Europe. Captions included the architect's name as well as the country and city location. While the series depicted structures from Norway, Spain, Denmark and France, a majority were from Germany and Austria-Hungary. From early 1913 until the series ended due to war, many images from Germany and Austria-Hungary, including Bohemia, showed designs of marked simplicity and an extreme sobriety of lines with little or no ornamentation. These included Josef Hoffmann's houses in the Hohe Warte area of Vienna as well as Paul Zimmerreimer's "Bal-Tabarin" on Jagerstrasse in Berlin. Also highlighted was Herman Muthesius's German country home that revealed a faint sense of "Englishness" with a rustic air of Teutonic linearity.[214] More importantly, the series proved that after 1912 British architects could not cop a plea of ignorance about cutting-edge Continental designs.

Interest in German designs became so important – for good reasons and bad – that in January 1914 the Art Standing Committee of the Royal Institute of British Architects recommended to the group's leadership that Hermann Muthesius present a paper at one of its monthly meetings on contemporary German architecture.[215] The beginning of the war later in the year prevented it from coming to fruition. If nothing else was absorbed by the burgeoning activity abroad, British architects realized how willing European colleagues were to experiment and take daring risks. While it remained

---

214 The series "Modern European Architecture" appeared in *Architect & Contract Reporter*. The designs emphasized appeared in the following issues: Hoffmann, 6 June 1913, p. 576; Zimmerreimer, 14 March 1913, p. 270; and Muthesius, 18 November 1910, p. 334.

215 "The Practice Standing Committee", Special Committee Minutes, Vol. 6 – November 4, 1910-February 10, 1914, 30 January 1914, pp. 443-444, *Royal Institute of British Architects Institutional Archives*. Collection stored at the Victoria and Albert Museum, London.

possible for some to doubt the longevity of the modern spirit, it became increasingly inconceivable to question its influence. The newly emerging world required a new architecture.

Ironically, *The Anglo-German Exhibition* held at the Crystal Palace from May-October 1913 epitomized the British reaction to the whirlwind of change in which it found itself. The exhibition also served as the last opportunity before the war for architects, artists and designers of both countries to exchange thoughts, proffer ideas and share professional courtesies with one another. Displays included commercial and industrial exhibitions, children's toys, sporting events and a lithography/poster display.[216] Opened by the Lord Mayor of London, the intent was "to promote amity and good feeling between the two nations" and it worked... up to a point. One critic hoped that the experience would not result in Britain adopting the more "famous forms" of German decoration. "Their originality is undoubted", he exclaimed, "but do we always like originality?"[217]

While no perfect reconciliation between the competing philosophies of architects seemed realistic, a *rapprochement* slowly emerged. Some expressed slim hope that the competing factions would tolerate each other's philosophy, and appreciate the importance of change and the necessity of accommodation. Many understood that while evolution took precedence over revolution, the continued reliance on historical tradition needed loosening. Architects who labored unceasingly within the rubric of authority and tradition needed to understand they could not disassociate art and design from popular taste or the demands of contemporary life. While accepting that vital architecture could not "spring from pandering to so-called popular tastes and demands", it also could never wholly be disassociated from them and still remain vital.

---

216 "The Crystal Palace Fund – An Anglo-German Exhibition", *The Times*, 12 June 1913, p. 4.

217 "The Anglo-German Exhibition", *The Builder*, Vol. CIV, 18 April 1913, p. 449.

"Architecture is no longer an aristocratic art", wrote the editors of *The Architects' & Builders' Journal,* "[and] it is not possible to uphold the divorce between art and the common people".[218] The times had changed. The once secure patronage of wealthy clients building new homes or expanding existing country estates was diminishing. Architects needed to understand the predispositions of society and appreciate the fledgling democratic impulse. If they failed, the profession would find itself inevitably trapped in a deep wilderness. "The opportunities of a very different order of art are but just dawning", reflected noted author and journalist, March Phillipps. "The demand of modern life is for an architecture direct and simple, strictly adapted to the purposes for which it is designed, and entirely emancipated from artificiality and affectation".[219] For Phillipps and countless others these changes surfaced because of the "democratic impulse" occurring throughout society.[220]

> The reversion of modern life from aristocratic to democratic is making it impossible for the stately Renaissance to subsist among us. Already it feels the breaking up under its feet of all that once supported it. The courtly etiquette and love of display which gloried in suites of gilded apartments and a coldly formal ostentation have quite departed. The opportunities of the architrave and pediment, of acanthus leaved capital and classic friezes are gone… instead the opportunities of a very different order of art are but just dawning.[221]

---

218 F. M., "Authority and the Modern Spirt", *The Architects' & Builders' Journal,* Vol. 39, 22 April 1914, pp. 276-277.

219 March Phillipps, "Modern Architecture and the Craftsman", *The Builder,* Vol. CV, 10 October 1913, pp. 359-360.

220 Arthur Stansfield Dixon, "Sources of Inspiration in Modern Art", *Journal of the Royal Institute of British Architects,* Vol. XV, No. 3, 1908, pp. 415-416.

221 March Phillipps, "Modern Architecture and the Craftsman", *The Builder,* Vol. CV, 10 October 1913, pp. 359-360.

While some feared the leveling momentum, others remained confident it would not run amok. "Modern style will evolve and invent features which are contrary to convenience or good construction", wrote architect Laurence Harvey, who had studied at Ecole des Beaux Arts, Paris. "But time will clip the wings of those who have gone mad with their newly acquired freedom, and there is hope that the 'modern style'… will bring us soon into a real wholesome state of art all over the world".[222] Architect James Sivewright Gibson, who designed primarily in the Gothic style and excelled at garnering public architectural competitions including Middlesex Guildhall in Westminster, took the long view, believing "architectural salvation" would be a difficult slog, but success would be achieved eventually. He lamented, however, the "hard-headed" and "practical approach" he and other architects had taken the past twenty-five years. Gibson wished more professionals had been "soft-headed, soft-hearted and unpractical" so they could have gloried in "our town, our city, our nation". Despite his disappointingly reflective tone Gibson offered encouragement for the future. "Our modest progress", he opined, "may bring the day nearer to those who will again rear up such architecture as will be an ennobling factor in the life of all who are privileged to see it".[223]

Despite the heady optimism of those clamoring for the "Modern Spirit" that offered individual expression and liberty, prudence required them to consider the futility of previous revolts. Followers of tradition reminded them that except for the monkish sentimentality of Gothic revival, the continuity of classic authority throughout history had remained unbroken. The Renaissance was a reversion to authority from the chaos of Medievalism, while the Jacobean and Georgian styles, argued traditionalists, were "the

222 Laurence Harvey, "Modern Style", *The Architect & Contract Reporter*, Vol. LXXXII, 10 September 1909, pp. 170-172.

223 James Sivewright Gibson, "Ideals in Architecture", *The Architect & Contract Reporter*, Vol. LXXXVII, 9 February 1912, pp. 99-100.

logical development of that hankering for the sane, the orderly, the authoritative…" [224]

The architectural debate again spread to *Punch*, the weekly magazine of satire. A late December 1910 issue featured two drawings: a rough sketch of a house desired by the client and another drawn by the architect and presented to the client. The differences between the two could not have been more dramatic. The client's sketch reflected a simple, straightforward design; however, the architect's rendering included a disparate hodgepodge of features reminiscent of several historical eras. While obviously humourous, it nevertheless demonstrated how society, at least those with the means to construct a new house, viewed architects and the profession as a whole.[225]

As progressives embraced the optimistic expressionism of the "Modern Spirit", stalwart traditionalists entrenched more deeply. The most dogmatic adherent was Reginald Blomfield, architect of numerous classical buildings throughout London and the last president of the Royal Institute of British Architects before the Great War. His inaugural address as well as arguments published twenty years later in *Modernismus* outlined the traditionalist's unalterable position. Contemporary art proved difficult to appreciate with real certainty, he exclaimed, because its historical longevity seemed doubtful. It was a folly perpetuated by camp followers and not genuine artists. "By refusing to study the art of the past, it starves its own techniques", Blomfield argued. "Its drawing is weak, its painting dull and meaningless, its modeling clumsy… and this comes of leaving the high-road and wandering about in dirty lanes and squalid alleys". Most discouraging to Blomfield was the tendency for modernisms to "minimize and disparage" the past. This axiom would prove extremely detrimental to architecture. Only by maintaining architecture's continuity with history, Blomfield believed, would

224 F. M., "Authority and the Modern Spirt", *The Architects' & Builders' Journal*, 22 April 1914, pp. 276-277.
225 "Charivari", *Punch*, Vol. CXXXIX, 28 December 1910, p. 451.

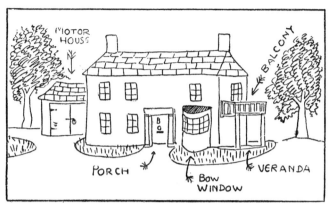

THIS IS THE ROUGH IDEA FOR HIS NEW HOUSE WHICH
MR. JONES GAVE TO HIS ARCHITECT.

AND THIS IS THE IDEA WHICH THE ARCHITECT THEN
GAVE TO MR. JONES.

Illustrations reproduced with permission of Punch Ltd., www.punch.co.uk

prevent a cataclysm similar to what Futurists and Cubists had perpetrated on fine art, sculpture and design. "It is time to give up conscious attempts at originality", Blomfield asserted, "… where our critics go wrong is in demanding a new language when they ought to be demanding new ideas. The old language will do very well if we are masters of it". Architecture was too serious an art form to abide in quick remedies to achieve originality. Blomfield blamed Germany and Austria for creating the subversive architectural movement that was nothing but a "crack remedy" for the chaos of the nineteenth century. The movement bordered on conspiracy, for modernisms' real intention, Blomfield declared, was to bankrupt all the arts. Its influences upon a new generation were dangerous and unhealthy because it promised a "wholly fallacious prospect of a new heaven on Earth" at the expense of studying the past. He encouraged wayward architects and impressionable students to avoid its degradation, ignore its narrowness of fashion, and return to the bedrock of traditionalism. Whatever the merits of contemporary French, German, and Austrian as well as American designs, Blomfield felt all were alien to British temperament. He strongly encouraged colleagues not to "allow its standards of value to be thrust aside by every impudent person who comes along with something new". Britain had an admirable tradition that had been ignored; however, with proper guidance, persistent study and patience it could be re-established. Moreover, despite the constant clamoring of its followers, modernisms could not be touted as the "herald of a new world" for its core was nothing but a "succession of false starts". Compromise, Blomfield believed, was impossible: modernisms had to be defeated or at a minimum quelled.[226]

---

226 Reginald Blomfield, "The Outlook of Architecture", *Journal of the Royal Institute of British Architects,* Vol. XXI, 1914, pp. 1-7. His ideas concerning modernisms were published later, but a majority of his ideas had been developed before the Great War and are included in this analysis. Reginald Blomfield, *Modernismus* (London: MacMillan & Co., 1934), pp. v-vi; 1-175; "Originality in Architecture", *The Architectural Review,* Vol. XXXIII, January-June 1913, p. 2.

On the eve of the Great War large segments of British society had failed to accept, let alone understand, artistic and architectural modernisms. In certain circles, including the Royal Institute of British Architects, serious discussions arose for expanding the public's appreciation for these disciplines. In mid-1913, the editors of *The Builder* appealed for the appointment of a Ministry of Fine Arts, believing it vitally necessary to increase the popular respect for the arts. "Whatever our differences are as to what constitutes artistic expression", the editors wrote, "… the cultivation of art is an important factor in the life and well-being of the body politic".

> The great want of art is to make itself understood by the people. To appeal to the dilettante and to convince the educated is only a part of the active work that must be done on behalf of the arts. The really vital necessity is to secure the hearty cooperation of many in order that they in turn may educate the people, for it is by popular understanding and appreciation that National Art which is worthy of the name must exist and have its being.[227]

The proposed ministry would consist of recognized authorities in architecture, painting and sculpture, and museums as well as industrial design. A dramatist, musician, literary author and antiquarian also would be included. Each specialist would advise the minister on aesthetic matters of public interest including national museums and galleries, modern national art, industrial art, and design alterations to cities, streets and public buildings. Additionally the ministry would be involved in preserving the amenities of towns, villages and the ever-diminishing countryside. Members would consult regularly with departments of the government requiring artistic advice. Supporters agreed that while society's taste had "undoubtedly improved", they thought – without

---

227 "An Appeal to Our Readers", *The Builder*, Vol. CV, 18 July 1913, p. 55.

listing specific examples – many past blunders and mistakes might have been avoided had a ministry of art existed. While most duties seemed straightforward, some thought the ministry also should offer advice on matters that "appear to require it".[228] While not announced publicly, such unchecked and undefined levels of power undoubtedly could be used to quarantine current or future modernist designs.

David Lloyd George responded quickly on behalf of Prime Minister Herbert Asquith stating that creating a new cabinet level position was not a "practical suggestion". Supporters remained undaunted as calls for a Ministry of Fine Arts continued to grow as the year progressed. Architectural author, H. Bartle Cox, enthusiastically supported the idea, arguing the world was experiencing a greater Renaissance than ever known in history. "In these days of easy transit, intercommunication, and foreign rapprochements", Cox continued, "international ideas are the more universal, and are tending towards greater peace and broader views... I would like to see a Ministry of Fine Arts established in England, so that our country could take its place with others in the education of the arts which are international".[229] The editors of *Burlington Magazine* thought the movement for a cabinet-level position reflected the increased importance of art throughout public life which in itself was a hopeful sign. And because the proposal coincided with a popular, contemporary belief of appealing to the state for the most complicated issues, the editors thought such a position might be an efficient remedy against the "recognized evils" in public activities.[230] The editors interestingly did not elaborate whether modernisms were included in any list of recognized evils. Perhaps that was why in late July 1914, amidst the turmoil of impending war, several members of both Houses

---

228 "A Ministry of Art", *The Builder*, Vol. CVI, 27 February 1914, p. 274.

229 H. Bartle Cox," Letter to the Editor", *The Builder*, Vol. CV, 8 August 1913, p. 143.

230 "Notes", *Burlington Magazine*, Vol. XXV, April-September 1914, p. 314.

of Parliament including Lord James Bryce, former Ambassador to the United States, and George Nathanial Curzon, The Earl Curzon of Kedleston, formed the Committee on Fine Arts. They believed a combination of apathy and ignorance had assailed the public's knowledge of and appreciation for architecture and art, and it was the Committee's goal to awaken and to elevate society's interest and broaden its comprehension of artistic matters. Members anticipated the government would act with such alacrity that a Ministry of Fine Arts would be added to the cabinet quickly.[231] World events, however, took precedence. The new cabinet office proposal simply vanished within the whirlwind of world war and was not discussed again for almost a decade.

The earlier pronouncement to create the definitive British-style architecture had become mired in grappling with and then combating the modern movement from Europe. Many architects thought modern designs from Germany and Austria, while curiously provocative, would join the pantheon of styles that had stifled creative advancement throughout the nineteenth century. Others, however, remained hesitant to discredit the movement so quickly. Introspective architects appreciated that tremendous cultural and societal changes were occurring throughout the Western world – from music and fine art to literature and architecture as well as an increased level of democracy. The inexplicable and unstoppable lust for change – the *zeitgeist* – held sway over many. Although intrigued by the idea of the "Modern Spirit" they could not quite rationalize how or why it had materialized but accepted its influence and attempted to operate within an altered paradigm.

Modernisms' quest to liberate society from conventionalized thought brought fierce and robust criticism from many architects

---

231 *The Architect & Contract Reporter*, Vol. XCII, 24 July 1914, p. 75. Other committee members included the following: Lord Crawford, A.A. Allen, Sir George Agnew, Lord Henry Bentinck, Sir Edward F. Coates, Stephen Gwynn, Sir Alfred Mond, Almeric Paget, Sir Gilbert Parker, Sir Herbert Raphael, Philip Snowden, Edward Wood and Montague Barlow.

and much of the public. Despite its haphazard diversities, two constants in modernisms were its defiance of authority and the abandonment of historical imperatives. Most modernists eagerly disassociated themselves from tradition, opting instead for the anti-traditional, ahistorical approach: a cavalier and rebellious attitude that not only ignored traditional art and architecture but traditional culture as well and thereby repudiated the entire historical continuum. This greatly disturbed society and helped raise reactionary rhetoric to higher levels. Although what became identified historically as "modern" had found fresh ground in Britain by the summer of 1914, there remained a lingering yet potent disgust at modernisms' perniciousness. The proposal for a new cabinet position – a Ministry of Fine Arts – was aimed partly at educating society while simultaneously controlling the more "unhealthy" infiltrations of modernisms into British culture. While the outrageous outbursts heard earlier in the century eventually were muffled, the centrifugal forces of world war soon crystallized a protracted aversion into a formidable intolerance.

4

A War Against Modernisms?

"In times of peace, art... becomes stereotyped and somnolent; it loses its initiative, it is thrown back upon itself, and it wastes its energies in petty squabbles. The rude shock of war makes it suffer, but out of the suffering there presently emerges a higher and more manly ideal, and the striving to realise this ideal leads to finer and more vital accomplishment".[232]

– The Studio, 1915

"For the modern German, whether we like his designs or not, has at least produced a modern architecture of distinctive character and different from any preceding architecture".[233]

– William R. Lethaby, Architect, 1915

---

232 "The Lay Figure: On Art and War", *The Studio*, Vol. 63, 1915, p. 80.
233 William R. Lethaby, "Lessons from Germany", *The Architect & Contract Reporter*, Vol. XCIII, 5 February 1915, pp. 115-116.

The vagaries of war affected Britain's architectural and artistic landscape immediately. What limited tolerance society had exhibited toward innovative cultural developments vanished with the war declaration. Britain quickly transformed its loathing of European modernisms into a jingoistic call to arms against the Central Powers. Despite numerous inconsistent messages, one predominated: to oppose Vorticist, Cubist or Futurist art became as patriotic as to oppose Germany. A plethora of critics, journalists, politicians and the public alike blindly linked most modernisms to Germany and Austria-Hungary and in so doing elevated new art and architecture to a patriotic bellwether. In many circles it became unpatriotic to advocate or to admire any modernist movement including the music compositions of Richard Strauss, Arnold Schönberg, Gustav Mahler and other modern German and Austrian composers. After war began, attempts were made to restrict all German classical music but such action quickly was considered impracticable. Such reactionary attitudes fueled the need to purge other foreign pestilences that had infiltrated British culture recently. For Vorticist artists like Wyndham Lewis, the "big bloodless brawl prior to the Great Bloodletting was over".[234] Ironically, the war upset society's reliance on the existing order – both more dramatically and more rudely – than any pre-war modernist movement ever could have done. On the first anniversary of the war's beginning, *The Builder* acknowledged that "all peoples [were] obsessed with the craving to be modern… [but] there is no longer that craving to slumber contentedly in the oceans of dreams, for the European conflict has electrified the world".[235] Whether real or imagined, the reassuring sunshine of the Edwardian Era had set.

The government took early advantage of the cauldron of hate that quickly developed for most things German. In his Queen's Hall

---

234 Percy Wyndham Lewis, *Blasting and Bombardiering, An Autobiography 1914-1926* (London: John Calder, 1982), p. 35.

235 "Modernism", *The Builder*, Vol. CIX, 9 July 1915, pp. 23-24.

speech of September 1914, Chancellor of the Exchequer David Lloyd George implied that the war had caused a new country – the real Britain – to emerge, free from the foreign indulgences of the past.

> There is something infinitely greater and more enduring which is emerging already out of this great conflict – a new patriotism, richer, nobler, and more exalted than the old. I see amongst all classes, high and low, shedding themselves of selfishness, a new recognition that the honour of the country does not depend merely on the maintenance of its glory in the stricken field, but also in protecting its homes from distress. It is bringing a new outlook to all classes. The great flood of luxury and sloth which had submerged the land is receding, and a new Britain is appearing. We can see for the first time the fundamental things that matter in life, and that have been obscured from our vision by the tropical growth of prosperity.[236]

Britain needed to return to its true self, according to Lloyd George, and discard all vestiges inessential to a life worth living or dying for.

In October 1914, Professor Selwyn Image, Slade Professor of Fine Art at Oxford, presented a paper to the Architectural Association in London titled "Art and War". He heartily embraced the war, believing it would serve as a purifying antidote to the cultural decadence that had consumed the nation for at least two decades. Society had trampled upon the artistic muse with meaningless trivialities, he argued. And the country's unhealthy acceptance of sumptuous luxuries replete with titillating novelties had created "a deep shallowness of judgment and sane appreciation". Image rejected the view of many who feared war would damage art. He believed a paradox existed: war and art were not always enemies,

---

236 David Lloyd George, *Speech Delivered by the Rt. Hon David Lloyd George, MP at the Queen's Hall London on September 19th, 1914* (London: Harrison and Sons, 1914), pp. 15-16.

and that peace – as evidenced by recent cultural history – was not always art's best friend. This war, more than any other conflict, Image implored, was about "fundamental ideals". He hoped it would provide "a salutary shock" to both art and overall conduct, for this truly was a "war to the finish, to the death".[237] Many of Image's compatriots shared his bellicose opinions: only fighting and winning would preserve a world without German *Kultur*.

Royal Academy professor of sculpture William Robert Colton's impassioned speech titled "The Effects of War on Art" typified wartime zealousness. Delivered in March 1916 at Carpenters' Hall, London, Colton reaffirmed his abhorrence to war but hoped the conflict would serve as a "violent tonic" for his diseased nation, helping it to separate the real from the fake by welding the country into one social unit. He thought the war might also purify British art that had fallen victim to European fads. Colton compared recent exhibitions to a "puffed-out and unhealthy fungus of enormous size, without beauty, without delicacy, and without health". He did not limit his disgust to fine art. To Colton, "[a] wave of diseased degeneracy had submerged philosophy, music, literature and art to such a depth that… future generations will gaze back with pity upon this period of mistaken morbidness". Although he believed wrongly that the movement's "viciousness" had been crystallized in Germany, Britain could not pretend exemption for it too had succumbed. Colton's wide casting of "mistaken morbidness" included architecture which also had exhibited some modernist eccentricities. Contemporary endeavors, he exclaimed, "had run a little off the rails in producing architecture without much intention".

We have elaborated the keystone to an awful extent. We use it without meaning and quite usually cut through

---

237 Selwyn Image, "Art and the War," *The Architect & Contract Reporter*, Vol. XCII, 30 October 1914, pp. 374-375.

lintels with it. We use arches without meaning simply as a decoration, and we use pillars where there is nothing and plinths and bases with nothing upon them. The pediment has long ceased to be the end of a gable, and is more or less used at the fancy of the architect.[238]

Despite his firm indictment of recent British designs, Colton admitted architecture fortunately had remained healthier than other cultural arts. He eagerly looked forward to architecture and art regaining some sanity when the sureness of peace returned. Countless others soon shared Colton's urge to destroy the foreignness that had infiltrated pre-war culture. This mission of destruction not only helped strengthen society's resolve to defeat the Central Powers, it may have fulfilled an important cultural necessity by becoming not only the first modern war, but also a war *against* modernisms.

Respected painter and etcher William Strang's speech, also delivered at Carpenters' Hall in early 1916, echoed sentiments similar to both Image and Colton. He felt war would purge society of its exotic sentiments and re-establish a wholesome and vigorous emotional sense that had been neglected for over a decade. As an original member of the Royal Society of Painter-Etchers, Strang expressed confidence that after victory art would return to portraying appealing and recognizable scenes from nature instead of the irrational arrangement and rearrangement of lines, forms, cubes and colours that lacked meaning. After all, reasoned Strang, man's earliest attempts at art – however primitive – had represented known objects. Artistic normalcy would return despite the insistence of Post-Impressionists and other inconsequential modernists who had abandoned history and continuity with the past.[239]

---

238 William R. Colton, "The Effects of the War on Art", *The Architect & Contract Reporter*, Vol. XCV, 17 March 1916, pp. 199-201.

239 William Strang, "Some Modern Movements in Painting", *The Architect & Contract Reporter*, Vol. XCV, 25 February 1916, pp. 145-147.

Aggressive jingoists soon found additional public outlets to spread their inaccurate messages. *The Times* titled its review of the *Second London Group Exhibition* in March 1915 as "Junkerism In Art", writing that

> such a display was essential to complete the chastening of our pride in twentieth-century civilisation. The war has shown that its possession does not necessarily endow the man of *Kultur* with higher moral sensibilities than a barbarian.

The reviewer concluded the specific works, which included Jacob Epstein's iconic *Rock Drill*, Wyndham Lewis's *The Crowd* and *Workshop* and C. R. W. Nevinson's *Returning to the Trenches* and *Ypres After the Second Bombardment,*

> revealed that the aesthetic tendencies of the most advanced school of modern art are leading us back to the primitive instincts of the savage… we can only call them Prussian in their spirit. These painters seem to execute a kind of goose-step, where other painters are content to walk more or less naturally. Perhaps if the Junkers could be induced to take to art, instead of disturbing the peace of Europe, they would paint so and enjoy it. They are not Prussian enough for their theories of art. They seem to have set their teeth firmly, and done their worst in a kind of aesthetic asceticism which prevents them from taking an interest in anything actual or concrete whatever. This asceticism seems now to have gone about as far as it possibly can go, and we only wonder what they will do next in the way of renunciation.[240]

---

240 "Junkerism In Art", *The Times*, 10 March 1915, p. 8.

Later in November 1915, when artist Mark Gertler exhibited *Creation of Eve* at the *Third London Group Exhibition*, a zealous patron placed a sign over her mid-section with the inscription, "Made in Germany".[241] Already finding modernism troublesome and irrelevant, the jingoistic press pounced on most artwork considered unpatriotic and subversive. The critic for the *Morning Post* amplified the Germanic connection by writing that the painting reflected a "Hunnish indecency".[242] Other newspapers joined the attack, accusing Gertler of being sensational, deliberately eccentric, impertinent and sacrilegious.[243] Although the public had difficulty understanding modern art prior to the war, any semblance of accepting it vanished with each posting of the "Roll of Honour". As the tally of the dead steadily increased anything remotely related to or reflecting German culture – whether accurate or not – came under fire. More incredible was the complete revision of the pre-war understanding that Post-Impressionist paintings were mainly of French origin. Now allied with France and in the throes of war, much of British society impulsively decided that modern art's genesis was not French but unmistakably German.

In his presentation to the Design and Industries Association in 1915, William R. Lethaby, ardent progressive even in the midst of world war, asked why Britain had abandoned its early leadership toward modernism. The vibrant modernizing process of the Arts and Crafts Movement had been a distinctly British affair of great promise but ended abruptly when architects relinquished all pretense of creating designs reflecting contemporary conditions. Instead they retrenched and copied what Lethaby termed disappointingly as the "catalogued" styles of the past – Greek,

---

241 Noel Carrington, editor, *Mark Gertler: Selected Letters* (London: Rupert Hart-Davis, Ltd., 1965), p. 106.

242 John Woodeson, *Mark Gertler: Biography of a Painter, 1891-1939* (London: Sidgwick & Jackson, 1972), p. 186.

243 Sarah MacDougall and Rachel Dickson, editor, *Uproar! The First 50 Years of the London Group* (London: Lund Humphries, 2014), p. 84.

Renaissance and Gothic revivals. Although widely imitated abroad, arts and crafts had struggled for a devoted following at home, Lethaby lamented, because critics practically destroyed the movement in its infancy. The movement had produced plenty of meaningful ideas including, as many have argued, sowing the seeds of early modernism that Germany, Austria-Hungary and other Continental rivals embraced and reworked.[244] "We ought to obtain far greater results from our own originality and initiative than we have done in the past", Lethaby urged. "We must learn to see the value of our own ideas before they are reflected back on us from the Continent".

They [the Germans] saw the essence of our best essays in furniture, glass, textiles, painting, and all the rest, and laying hold on them, coined them into money, while our press, caught up into an eddy of devilish bright writing, set about to kill the whole thing.

He thought it immaterial whether Britain "liked" German designs, for its architects had seized upon the theory of real architecture and "produced a modern architecture of distinctive character and different from any preceding architecture".[245] Lethaby's penetrating analysis unfortunately was lost on many colleagues who, in the fog of war, continued to view German and Austrian design innovations suspiciously.

Society continued to cleanse itself of pre-war trivialities and

---

244 In 1959 when Ludwig Mies van der Rohe accepted the Royal Institute of British Architect's Gold Medal for Architecture, he credited C. F. A. Voysey, Charles Rennie Mackintosh, Edwin Lutyens and M. H. Baillie-Scott as pioneers whose work he came to study fifty years earlier. Alan Powers, *Modern: The Modern Movement in Britain* (London: Merrell Publishers, 2005), pp. 10-17.

245 William R. Lethaby, "Design and Industry", *Form in Civilization: Collected Papers on Art and Labour* (London: Oxford University Press, 1957), pp. 38-53. He delivered the speech in January 1915. "Lessons from Germany", *The Architect & Contract Reporter*, Vol. XCIII, 5 February 1915, pp. 115-116.

steer toward honorable purposes as the severity of the war increased. The editors of *The Builder* reaffirmed Germany's connection to modernisms and dismissed it as a misnomer, a mere "caricature of old methods". Modern building innovations and unique designs could not make a structure "modern and beautiful" if the architect had not felt some of the "charm and nobility which is inseparable from the work of the past". Germany's newly fashioned architecture, acclaimed earlier for its "originality", "virility" and "strength", was viewed now as having alienated itself from the acknowledged order of things – tradition and history – and thereby had lost all charm.[246]

In 1915, author, writer and critic Saint John Greer Ervine offered a biting commentary when he compared the hedonistic Edwardian Era with the purposeful period of wartime.

That we shall hear no more of the pretty-pretty babblers, with their Bond Street barbarism and their rococo recklessness. The Vorticists and the Imagists and the Futurists and the rest of the rabble of literary and artistic lunatics provided slender entertainment for empty days; but our minds are empty no longer; and we have no time to waste on monkeys on sticks.[247]

An ex-patriot living in Deauville, France, urged a return to the exquisiteness of nature and an end to the repellent, grotesque and

---

246 "Modernism", *The Builder*, Vol. CIX, 9 July 1915, pp. 23-24.

247 St John Ervine, "The War and Literature", *North American Review*, July 1915, p. 98. Despite the vitriolic commentary, late in the war humour managed to find its way, however fleetingly, into the discussion when a British architectural journal found that a U.S. Army lieutenant had written an article about the history of camouflage. The goal was to "screen operations, falsify the layout and confuse the landscape" as well as use "forms and colours that will deceive not only the eye, but the camera also". He then asked rhetorically: "But is not the Futurist already adept at camouflage, the art of making things seem confusing other than they are?" "The Development of Camouflage", *The Architectural Review*, Vol. 43, January-June 1918, p. xvii.

angular shapes that had monopolized the art world recently. He stated sarcastically that after the war, in order to combat the poisons Cézanne and his ilk had unleashed on society, it should "reproduce, as an antidote, the astounding work of the Cro-Magnon [sic] draughtsmen of wild beasts made in the caves of Altamira 20,000 years before the Christian era".[248] Such strong medicine, the ex-patriot insisted, undoubtedly would wipe out the last vestiges of the contagion. Even during wartime such cynical humour demonstrated society's preoccupation with foreign cultural movements that had percolated years before.

It was the war paintings of Britain's only committed Futurist, C. R. W. Nevinson, that dramatically altered – if only temporarily – public sentiment toward purging society of new art. His 1916 exhibition, *Paintings and Drawings of War* at London's Leicester Galleries, depicted the pitiable reality of modern warfare by using stark, angular and modern sensitivities. Nevinson's unique interpretations based on experiences as a motor mechanic and ambulance driver at the front surprisingly impressed the critics, enabling Charles Lewis Hind to write:

> He is an artist, a fighting artist, who has rampaged like a 'Tank' through all the modern movements; he has bustled through Impressionism, Post Impressionism, Cubism, Vorticism; and out of Cubism he has brought to birth a curious geometrical formula, sharp and glittering as a sword, which is admirably suited to his vision of this scientific, mechanical war.[249]

---

248 Ralph Curtis, Letter to the Editor, "Les Fauves", *Burlington Magazine*, Vol. XXXI, 1917, pp. 123-124.

249 Charles Lewis Hind, "True War Pictures. Mr. Nevinson's Moralities at the Leicester Galleries", *The Daily Chronicle*, 30 September 1916. One detractor was Ezra Pound who, holding an earlier grudge between his beloved Vorticists and the Futurists, chidingly believed the masses had come to "see" the war and not the art. Pound argued that Nevinson's work did not offer anything new.

His works also influenced senior military personnel and government officials. Sir Ian Hamilton, commander of the disastrous Gallipoli campaign, wrote the catalogue's introduction, extolling the virtue of the canvases as if to validate Nevinson's interpretations of his own combat experiences. Some exhibition pieces eventually became iconic images of the war including *La Mitrailleuse*, *La Patrie* and *Bursting Shell*.[250]

Ridding British society of pre-war modernisms was not the sole topic of conversation. In the midst of world war, discussions arose about the future of architecture and art after certain victory. Two broad but conflicting views predominated. One involved ending the "cult of ugliness" in architecture by reattempting to define the distinctive British style and restoring the reliance on classical tradition in art.[251] In his address to the Architectural Association, Albert E. Richardson, architect, prolific author and passionate devotee of the 18th century, admitted "the whole complexion of things" would change as a result of war, but the outlook for individuals and nations would "broaden to a deeper understanding of life". He hastened to add, however, that the war's outcome would bring about a chastening spirit that invariably would benefit architecture.[252] The opposing but progressive faction embraced the burgeoning modern spirit, eagerly anticipating an unpredictable golden age not shackled to Victorian/Edwardian revivalism and tradition. To many, the war would purify – if not destroy – the old order and anoint a new era clamoring to be born.

Surprisingly, modernist writer, poet and ex-soldier Richard Aldington believed that war hysteria probably would purge most recent art. When the carnage ended, he wrote a bit flippantly,

---

250 Michael J. K. Walsh, *Hanging a Rebel: The Life of C. R. W. Nevinson* (Cambridge: The Lutterworth Press, 2008), p. 114. The exhibition proved so popular it was extended a week.

251 "Art After the War", *The Architect*, Vol. XCL, 16 June 1916, p. 427.

252 "The Architectural Spirit of the Age", *The Architect & Contract Reporter*, 26 February 1915, pp. 186-189.

"things" would be different. "Possibly there will be no art at all – very probably, I should think. Anyway, lots of the cranky stuff of the last few years will be swept away".[253] Several others shared Aldington's analysis that the war would serve as a tremendous yet incalculable watershed for the cultural arts.

Many art critics were convinced in an almost self-fulfilling manner that new art definitely would be a casualty. Its inherent rebelliousness and subversiveness simply would not survive the upheavals brought by the war. While admitting it impossible to predict an exact date, they expressed confidence that representational art – portraying recognizable objects and natural images – would triumph. Art had lost initiative prior to the war. It had become stereotyped. Self-absorbed artists had made it somnolent. The war's purifying fire would end not only the petty squabbles about artists' style, emotion and intent but also would produce higher, more vital and finer work. Attaining a harmonious cooperation was vitally important even if it meant subjugating the individual to the organization. They hoped for a restoration of pre-war artistic ideals when peace arrived, blissfully unaware of or deliberately ignoring the breadth and genesis of new art.[254] To ensure this occurred they resurrected the idea of creating a Ministry of Fine Arts, first proposed days before Britain declared war. Such an office would evoke public interest in architecture and art by fighting ignorance and enhancing artistic quality by establishing exacting standards.[255]

---

253 Richard Aldington, "Notes on the Present Situation", *The Egoist*, No. 17, Vol. 1, 1 September 1914, p. 326.

254 William Strang, "Some Modern Movements in Painting", *The Architect & Contract Reporter*, Vol. CX, 25 February 1916, pp. 145-147; "The Lay Figure: On Art and War", *The Studio*, Vol. 63, 1915, p. 80; "Art After the War", *The Architect*, Vol. XCL, 16 June 1916, p. 427.

255 "An Appeal to Our Readers", *The Builder*, Vol. CV, 18 July 1913, p. 55; *The Architect & Contract Reporter*, 24 July 1914, p. 75; "The Architectural Spirit of the Age", *The Architect & Contract Reporter*, 26 February 1915, pp. 186-189. In 1915-1916, the Royal Institute of British Architects had hoped to have a member present a paper at one of its meetings on a Ministry of Fine Arts but it never occurred.

In late 1914, *The Builder* offered a different viewpoint in its editorial, "War and the Arts". The war would cause neither a renaissance in the arts or a return to tradition. The editors reasoned that around 1906 or 1907 the arts had become both more "serious in intention" and "more valuable in content". It would be wrong to assume that if the movement's effervescence continued after the war, the war caused the change. "The germs of it were there long before the war was thought of", the editor wrote. The war might alter superficial forms of expression but it would not move art forward. In fact, the editor confessed that "neither victor nor vanquished" ever come out of war better off than when they went in. Perhaps more importantly the editor emphasized that "for good or ill" modern art, architecture, music and literature would not disappear after the war. Modernisms would survive and demand from the public a higher level of education and culture and, in all likelihood, would not appeal to the ignorant. Pseudo-elitism would triumph over democratization.[256] The *Observer* echoed similar sentiments, arguing that the honoured masters of tomorrow ironically could be the reviled Post-Impressionists, Cubists, Futurists, Expressionists and Vorticists of today.[257] Both journals surprisingly were correct. Modernism, replete with its transformative nature, thrived in the post-war era.

As early as 1915, articles appeared predicting that dramatic change was afoot for both art and society. *The Studio's* recurring column "The Lay Figure" addressed numerous themes a post-war society would face. Several predictions proved quite prescient.

> The change will come in the course of time and will be due to the activity of the younger generation; as that grows up it will oust... the older men... The younger generation

---

256 "War and the Arts", *The Builder*, Vol. CVII, 13 November 1914, pp. 443-444.

257 Robert Graves and Alan Hodge, *The Long Week-end: A Social History of Great Britain 1918-1939* (New York: W. W. Norton & Company, 1963), p. 192.

will not be content with the ideas of their grandfathers. The young men who have faced the definite facts of life for themselves will have developed their own views and will want to express them in their own way. And there will be a new public, also acquainted with the facts of life, which will be prepared to accept these views. But what we do not know is whether the art which is to satisfy these artists and this new public will be better or worse in character and quality than the art which has sufficed for us hitherto... Art in the years to come may have to begin again and to fight its way up to a safe and stable position, but it will do so by wholesome means. The *new spirit* may make it brutal and uncompromising, or may make it abstract and imaginative, but certainly will require it to be clean. The primitive passions which lie beneath the surface of civilisation have been aroused and they, just because they are freed from any taint of artificiality, are out of sympathy altogether with decadence.

The article acknowledged it could not predict what form art would take, but it would not continue along the old lines. "The old order is most surely passing away", the editors argued, "and it is altogether obvious that new conditions must produce new results, though these results may be slow in making their appearance".[258]

Roger Fry encouraged change but felt it necessary to temper his enthusiasm. In a speech delivered to the Fabian Society Summer School in 1917 titled "The New Movement in Art in its Relation to Life", he celebrated new art's success in altering the broader landscape, but remained undecided whether there would be a corresponding transformation in overall thought and feeling about life throughout society. He hazarded to speculate whether the differences – if there were any – between the 19th and 20th centuries would seem as

---

258 "The Lay Figure: On the Art that May Be", *The Studio*, Vol. 63, 1915, p. 318.

great in everyday life as they did already in the art world. Despite sounding pessimistic, Fry hoped a similar attitude would infiltrate post-war society. Fry feared the new movements unfortunately had transitioned artists and their art into an obscure sphere too remote for ordinary people to understand or to appreciate. "In proportion as art becomes pure the number of people to whom it appeals gets less. It cuts out all the romantic overtones of life", Fry stated, "which are the usual bait by which the work of art induces men to accept it". Because art appealed to aesthetic sensibilities which, Fry lamented, were incredibly weak among most men, it had lost wider acceptance and become irrelevant.[259]

Fry's friend and close associate, Clive Bell, believed passionately that "even a European war" could not destroy the modern movement. He thought the direct opposite: all the evidence indicated a strong vibrancy. While adversaries had complained for years about the foreignness of new art and continued to do so throughout the war, Bell argued the reverse. In fact, he lamented the current state of homegrown British art. The traditionally provincial British artists, who never had looked to Europe for inspiration, needed to embrace alternative influences if they hoped to reach beyond the banality of amenity art. "There is no live tradition", Bell argued, "and as English painters refuse obstinately to accept the European, and as artists do not spring up unaccountably as groundsel and dandelions appear to do, the defect is serious". Bell argued that an art student studying in any great European city – from Paris, Stockholm, Moscow and Munich to Vienna, Geneva, Barcelona and Milan – could discuss the contemporary movements and argue the merits of Henri Matisse, Pablo Picasso, Andre Derain, Andre Segonzac or Robert Delaunay. They also could criticize their work, know what direction their works were taking, and appreciate the varied influences on their art. "Only in an English studio", Bell conceded

---

259 Roger Fry, "The New Movement in Art in its Relation to Life", *Burlington Magazine*, Vol. XXXI, July 1917, pp. 162-168.

tersely, "would such conversation be hard to come by". Bell was equally disappointed that patronage of the arts amounted to "an expensive pleasure" of the rich, well-born and the good. To make matters worse, anyone remotely interested in art had to look to them who, Bell exclaimed, "have no use either for art or for good painting", for criticism, sympathy and understanding.

Although Bell was a fervent new art advocate who lauded the work of Duncan Grant and Jacob Epstein, he had concerns. Bell criticized Wyndham Lewis who, as a Bloomsbury outsider, was canalizing the new spirit toward the backwater of Vorticism. Its insipid provincialism drained the modern spirit of vitality making it both impotent and insignificant. He implored Britain's artists "to wake up after the war and take their place in a league of nations" and appreciate by reason of vocation that they belonged to a community both wider and more significant than their own. Bell encouraged them not to mimic their predecessors who, he wrote, "appear to have preferred being pygmies amongst cranes to being artists amongst artists".[260]

It was too early in summer 1918 to determine whether the *Observer*, *The Studio*, Roger Fry or Clive Bell correctly understood the path new art would take after the war, but the fact that *Punch* published a parody featuring Futurism demonstrated the country's continued uneasiness surrounding modern art movements in general. For the farmers of Great Britain, Brink's patented Futurist scarecrow, designed by an 'eminent Cubist', practically guaranteed birds would not fly within three fields of it. A farmer and a member of the Women's Land Army stare inquisitively at the design, either marveling at or mocking its composition.[261] The cartoon's appearance could be interpreted two ways. It may have served as a reminder that the miserable charade of pre-war art would end only with a defeated

---

260 Clive Bell, "Contemporary Art in England", *Burlington Magazine*, Vol. XXXI, July 1917, pp. 30-37.

261 "The London Charivari", *Punch*, Vol. CLC, 17 July 1918, p. 33.

Germany, or conversely may have indicated the permanence of new art movements even after Britain achieved victory. Regardless of the interpretation, there was little doubt that the persistence of modernisms preyed on society's war-weary conscience. Ironically, the drawing appeared during the Allies' great summer offensive that by October-November had turned the tide of war, enabling the guns to fall silent at 11:00 am on 11 November 1918.

Traditionalist architects hoped that when peace returned building designs would incorporate precedent as the irrefutable foundation for anything new. The plea for a distinctively British style of architecture unencumbered by foreign influences re-emerged, having been dormant for almost a decade as the fracas surrounding modernisms had intensified. Many encouraged Britain to return to its traditions where regional requirements and purposes could render a distinctive and meaningful architecture. Sculptor William R. Colton, who soon would serve as President of the Royal British Society of Sculptors, hoped for a sane future when peace came, and pleaded with colleagues to "[l]et us make things as beautiful as we can, let us make things as healthy as we can".[262]

The Builder went further and discarded German designs altogether. Their influences would not survive the war.

> The German temperament is essentially an initiative one and its desperate efforts at originality, so persistent as to show that it feels its own lack, have resulted in the bizarre and uncouth rather than in any fresh and striking forms of beauty. We have been so hypnotised by the repeated Teutonic statement of Teutonic genius that in some quarters we have perhaps allowed ourselves to take the vagaries of modern architecture in Germany more seriously than they deserved.

---

262 William R. Colton, "The Effects of War on Art", *The Architect & Contract Reporter*, Vol. XCV, 17 March 1916, pp. 199-201.

The editors hoped that after victory Britain would emerge from its aimless wondering and develop its own architectural style: "It will be a thousand pities if we allow our just admiration for a very great nation to obscure the lonely furrow which we must plough if we are again to count as a nation with an architectural style of its own".[263] Sharing this point of view were architects who without hesitation relegated the once highly lauded Otto Wagner, Josef Hoffmann and Peter Behrens as mere "new art specialists of our own yester-year".[264]

The war had an almost redemptive impact on those who embraced modernisms. It offered limitless opportunities to contemplate a dynamic age for an architecture unencumbered by history. A return to the bankrupt days before the war dominated by creative immobility seemed unlikely. The constricting shackles of imitation and decoration soon would be unlocked. "Economy of construction will create a sobering and restrained effect upon style", wrote Harold G. Leask, an architect passionate about archeology and historical architecture. He hoped exterior walls would no longer be festooned with swags, wreaths, cartouches, sculpturesque infants and females galore on every vacant piece of wall space and protruding from every angle. Leask encouraged architects after the war to concentrate on designing a quality structure in the "proper and most important position".[265] It was imperative for architects to expand their horizons and to emancipate the profession from its "insular apathy". "It is essential", Albert E. Richardson wrote, "that we as English architects… enjoy an enlarged vision of architectural achievement in other countries, and to profit by the experience".[266]

---

263 "War and the Arts", *The Builder*, Vol. CVII, 13 November 1914, pp. 443-444.

264 "An Estimate of German Architecture", *The Architectural Review*, Vol. XLI, January-June 1917, pp. 20-21. The author sheepishly admitted, however, that they "probably… did some good."

265 Harold G. Leask, "The War and Architecture", *The Architect & Contract Reporter*, Vol. XCIV, 31 December 1915, pp. 506-507. Presidential address delivered before the Architectural Association of Ireland.

266 Albert E. Richardson, "The Architectural Spirit of the Age", *The Architect & Contract Reporter*, Vol. XCIII, 26 February 1915, pp. 186-189.

Eight days before the Armistice Henry T. Hare, architect of several public libraries throughout the country and president of the Royal Institute of British Architects, addressed colleagues at the opening of the organization's General Meeting. The profession and the nation were on the threshold of a new era. "Our whole system and scheme of life have been dislocated and virtually destroyed", Hare reflected. "We have the opportunity of making a new beginning and it is for us to approach the complex problems which face us with open minds anxious to build upon a sure and solid foundation… "[267] And so, as the carnage ended the challenging burden for those who survived the war had become self-evident. While the problems had been present years, if not decades, before, by the end of the war there could be little denying that the old ways lacked relevancy.

To Robert Burns Dick of Newcastle-upon-Tyne and Northern Architectural Association president, the war had forced Britain to enter the opening phases of a new Renaissance. "The flickering fire of the classical Renaissance is on the wane", Dick exclaimed, "and another torch is about to be ignited at its dying embers… [but] who amongst the nations will or can clasp it if not Imperial Britain". Only Britain was worthy of this "great trust".[268] Dick remained optimistic even as the horrors of war raged. He felt confident that when the crisis concluded a golden age would emerge, forging a distinctive style of architecture from which the new era would become identified. Active in community life and possessing abundant amounts of civic pride – his most well-known structure, the Cornish granite twin pylons on each side of the Tyne Bridge in Newcastle (1928) remained in the future – he believed the war was directly responsible for launching a new order: "It will materially change the citizen's outlook in a way nothing else could have done". Architects also would have to

267 Henry T. Hare, "Address by the President", *Journal of the Royal Institute of British Architects*, Vol. XXVII, 4 November 1918, pp. 1-5.
268 R. Burns Dick, "War and Architecture", *Journal of the Royal Institute of British Architects*, Vol. XXII, 25 November 1914, pp. 83-90.

contribute. With an increased intelligence and widened outlook by society, architecture would take its proper place amongst the important things desired in life. "A higher standard of attainment will be demanded of architects than in the past", Dick predicted, "and only those of us who are worthy of it may hope for success in the Golden Age to come".[269]

Dick's zealousness greatly intensified after victory. Knowingly or accidentally, he sprinkled elements of Italian Futurism in his February 1919 address to the Northern Architectural Association.

> We have learned the secret of perpetual youth. It is for us, if we will, to weave ourselves into the pattern of this Greater Renaissance, and just as long as time we are indissolubly one with it; we are immortal… Let us get rid of the old shibboleths, the old prejudices, the petty rivalries, the unworthy jealousies, the disproportionate sense of our own dignity, the too sensitive solicitude of our *armour propre*, the cynicism of disillusion – disappointed hopes, and all the devil's brood that we are prone at times to consort with.

Despite delivering such a romantic and idealistic pronouncement, Dick understood earlier than most that the war had caused fundamental changes and the nation needed to adapt. He argued that national reconstruction involved reconstituting every institution that contributed to national life and character. And architecture, by its very nature, could not be neglected by society, nor could architects ignore an altered world. The profession had become so self-centered before the war that a creeping paralysis had caused a severe loss of appreciation amongst architects and within the broader community. The war had destroyed the sophistries of the Victorian and Edwardian eras and what had emerged in its stead

---

269 Robert Burns Dick, "The Cataclysm – And After", *Journal of the Royal Institute of British Architects*, Vol. XXIV, 9 December 1916, pp. 39-40.

was a dramatically different country. Dick thought it incumbent upon the profession that it

> ... must now aggressively demonstrate that side of our work that will appeal to the work-a-day mind – that the problems involved in fitting the structures of our time to the needs that arise, and in facilitating the smooth flow and development of industrial and social life, are just those that our training is designed to solve, but in addition, that in the solving of these problems we can be trusted to give an expression that will satisfy and draw out and inspire the higher and spiritual side of our people's dual nature.

Dick felt confident that, despite the incumbent challenges of the post-war era, architects should "give rein to our imagination as a preliminary to a greater and more far reaching understanding of the demands of a practical world". The aftermath of war had revealed the failures from the past which had taken a toll on faith and obscured enthusiasm. But a rebirth had occurred and with it the surging optimism of youth. Dick implored his colleagues to embrace the future, encouraging them to design and to build for today with an eye toward tomorrow, not yesterday.

> Away with the dead things of the Past! We are the living Past. Look to the Future! We are the Future in the making. The time is ripe. Let us build well, with an eye to the requirements not only of our time but to those of the future. No doubt our work will have to give way before the march of progress, but how long it will last will depend upon the breadth and depth of our vision. [270]

---

270 Robert Burns Dick, "The Greater Renaissance", *Journal of the Royal Institute of British Architects*, Vol. XXVI, February 1919, pp. 83-84.

Many shared Dick's optimism about the future. The horribleness of war necessitated creating a society better than the one that had given birth to the devastation.

By early autumn 1918, the assurance of victory allowed both factions to feel that change was near if not inevitable. Supporters of architectural and artistic modernisms remained convinced that a new Renaissance soon would unfold. Change appeared palpable and unequivocal. It seemed implausible that society and the cultural arts would return to a pre-1914 level of existence. Many in Britain hoped for the opposite. The country would return to the way it had been prior to the war, void of materialistic extravagances and the uncomfortable foreignness of modernisms. They lacked any incentive for changing the cultural outlook, desiring instead a return to normalcy. The enormous cost for victory – in terms of lives lost and the damaged psychological underpinnings of society – created the expectation that a pre-1914 standard seemed warranted. As time progressed it became obvious that significant portions of their respective assumptions would remain unrealized. The war had robbed modernisms of its youthful vibrancy and had snuffed out any relevancy to the past.

5

Out of the Abyss Emerged a New Reality

"The movement towards a modern architecture is not new in England; but it has required the war and the example of other countries to open up the development of a spirit which originated very largely on English soil but which was repressed by conservatism and the lack of sequence in early effort".[271]

– Howard Robertson, Architect, 1925

"We believe that the whole of works of the post-impressionists, futurists, and cubists in painting will in a hundred years, or even less, be considered as being worth the value of the canvas they are painted on, and no more, though they well may be the work of men who, had they

---

271 Howard Robertson, "Modern Architecture of the North", *Journal of the Royal Institute of British Architects*, Vol. XXXII, 7 March 1925, pp. 273-280. Paper delivered before the Architectural Association of Ireland on 17 February 1925.

chosen saner methods, might have achieved lasting fame and reputation, and that a similar fate may well be that of many works by modern writers".[272]

– The Architect, 1925

After the carnage ended and peace assured, widespread disillusion dominated war-weary psyches. Marion Harry Spielmann, art critic, publisher and prolific author who unsurprisingly had shunned modern art earlier in the century, wrote *The Times*, lamenting the unhealthy state of British society.

> [W]e have seen much the same eccentricities in all the arts within quite recent years – in architecture as in sculpture, in painting, poetry, music, costume as well as in religious and spiritual exercises, and in social life and manners. We have, in fact, been passing through... the poison belt of dementia of which the maddest and crowning symptom has been the Great War itself. We must recognize the tragic truth – realize that when the world and its inhabitants recover their equilibrium, and not before, will men – artists and others – awaken to the absurdities and horrors under which we are groaning. Not the greatest of these are the deterioration in architecture and the disorientation of certain artists and writers on art. They are but a symptom, not the disease.[273]

Spielmann's depressed tone and lingering dissatisfaction reflected the feelings of many throughout Britain. In the immediate post-war period society unsurprisingly acted as it had before the war. There was a return to order, a desire for normalcy. It rebuked the distorted and

272 "Modern Art in Industry", *The Architect*, Vol. CXIV, 9 October 1925, pp. 249-250.

273 Marion Harry Spielmann, "Modern Art, Architecture and the Critics", *The Times*, 25 May 1920, p. 6.

misshapen forms, shapes and colours in paintings; the meandering dissonance in music; the nonsensical, sound-before-sense poetry; and the dull, over-decorated and expressionless architecture.[274] Some historians contend a certain level of disenchantment had been present long before, growing steadily throughout the early 20th century. The war and its aftermath only magnified the feeling.[275]

In the war's aftermath, the word *zeitgeist* ceased being used to explain the momentous cultural changes Britain had experienced before 1914. The war killed its usage along with other cultural certainties, causing many to believe the *zeitgeist* had presaged human destruction and not pointed toward cultural advancement. And so it made perfect sense that immediately after victory society discarded any symbols of modernisms, preferring instead the delusory comforts of the past and the enduring appeal of the classical and historical tradition. How to return to the basic fundamentals of life preoccupied combatants and non-combatants alike.

Architect Ernest Newton, who had apprenticed with Richard Norman Shaw in the late 19th century, was a founder member of the Art Workers' Guild and had served as president of the Royal Institute of British Architects during the most trying time of the war from 1914-1917, confidently believed the country would return to a pre-1914 form of cultural normalcy.[276] Similar to his colleagues, Newton failed to appreciate the far-reaching ramifications of war. Newton expressed his views in an article co-authored with Walter Godfrey published in *Architectural Review* soon after the Versailles Treaty was signed in June 1919. While public monuments certainly would call attention to the noble sacrifice of the soldiers, Newton

---

274 "Present Day Art Tendency", *The Architect*, Vol. CXI, 20 June 1924, p. 440. The article commented on a story titled "Problems of the Home" that appeared in the magazine *Women*.

275 Andrew Frayn, *Writing Disenchantment: British First World War Prose, 1914-1930* (Manchester: Manchester University Press, 2014), p. 201.

276 Ernest Newton Obituary, *Journal of the Royal Institute of British Architects*, Vol. XXIX, 28 January 1922, p. 191.

thought architecture would continue inappreciably affected by four years of carnage. He believed wholeheartedly in re-establishing architecture's pre-war conditions. "I do not think that our life has been so much modified by the war that any great difference will be required in the planning of country houses", he wrote confidently. The only issue that would impinge upon architects would be the severe shortage of servants, for "[i]t is likely… ", Newton continued, "that for some time to come, instead of the demand for 'cupboards', so well known to architects, the demand will be for 'labour-saving appliances'. I venture to suggest that the best labour-saving device is for everybody to do some housework herself".[277] Newton's over-simplification was partially correct. There was a wholesale decrease in household staff but the largest reduction occurred in middle-class homes, not only in the homes of the wealthy, upper classes.[278] It was perhaps unfathomable for Newton, a renowned and prolific architect of country houses and devotee of architectural education, to comprehend the far-reaching social and cultural upheavals that emerged in the aftermath of the Great War.

Newton's colleague, building conservationist and architectural historian, Walter H. Godfrey, contributed the second part of the article by arguing that architecture would best be served if it reflected the enormous gains garnered by victory. "[T]he completeness of the victory over the most unscrupulous enemy known to history", Godfrey stated, "makes it morally certain that Europe will draw from it a robust health, a casting-off of the strange pre-war *migraine*; and in this restoration of virility we may hope to witness an important revival of architectural art". He admitted the difficulty in predicting how Britain would react. The British establishment was largely adverse to creative artistry while the intellectual element was "strangely anti-national". Despite the dichotomy, Godfrey believed

---

277 Ernest Newton, "Peace and the Art of Architecture, Part I", *The Architectural Review*, Vol. XLVI, July-December 1919, pp. 160-161.

278 Arthur Marwick, *The Deluge: British Society and the First World War* (Boston: Little, Brown and Company, 1965), p. 303.

Britain had too big a share in the war to escape its "energizing influence" and may actually lead rather than follow other nations toward developing an architecture that reflected the hard-fought victory.[279] Time proved Godfrey incorrect on both predictions: Britain failed to lead any movement and most, if not all, post-war architecture struggled to reflect any semblance of victory.

Pre-war avant-garde artists retrenched after the war, pursuing more conservative styles than they had done previously. Human figures suddenly became more recognizable. "The war was a sleep, deep and animal", wrote artist Wyndham Lewis. "Upon waking I found an altered world. The geometries which had interested me so exclusively before, I now felt were bleak and empty. They wanted filling".[280] While some felt the war had created, as poet Siegfried Sassoon acerbically lamented, "a cemetery for the civilized delusions of the nineteenth century",[281] the majority of society believed the road to recovery and restoration was not paved with modernisms but the "backward glance", the delusory comforts of the atavistic Edwardian Era. It would be almost a decade before many discovered that the war, as Virginia Woolf reflected later, had "destroyed illusion and put truth in its place".[282]

The desire to return to a pre-war Britain seemed also to have occurred in politics. War leader David Lloyd George remained Prime Minister by forming a new Coalition government after winning the late November 1918 election. The Treasury reasserted its control under the leadership of Austen Chamberlain who resumed the position he first held in 1903. Lord Curzon presided over the

---

279 Walter H. Godfrey, "Peace and the Art of Architecture, Part II", *The Architectural Review*, Vol. XLVI, July-December 1919, pp. 160-161.

280 Michael Glover, "In the Mind of the Draughtsman", *The Financial Times*, 21 December 2004, p. 14.

281 Siegfried Sassoon, *The Weald of Youth* (London: Faber and Faber Limited, 1922), p. 274.

282 Virginia Woolf, *A Room of One's Own* (London: Penguin Group, 2000), pp. 23-24.

Foreign Office, and former Foreign Secretary and Prime Minister Arthur Balfour, having returned from the Congress of Berlin, served as Lord President of the Council. Such political continuity caused Douglas Jerrold, avid Conservative, journalist and future editor of *The English Review*, to comment years later about whether time had stood still: "No wonder that no one knew... whether we were going on or going back".[283] Unsurprisingly the war had the opposite effect on Germany and the former Austria-Hungary. Because the defeated Central Powers blamed the past for the calamity and the respective governments and monarchies they supported no longer existed, they willingly embraced anything that appeared new, different, modern and progressive.

The comforting sureness of tradition first emerged in mediating bereavement. As Jay Winter has argued, modernisms portrayed anger quite effectively but they could not mend or repair, forcing the living to seek solace in classical, romantic or religious forms, not modern.[284] The task to memorialize the fallen was not new. It had started strangely enough when war began, gradually melding into a larger debate on what path post-war architecture would take. Architects may have been the first to discuss the designs as well as potential messages the memorials should convey. "There must be no niggardly dealing in connection with it", wrote the editors of *The Architectural Review* in early 1915. "Isolated statues and mediocre tablets will not suffice to record the terrific nature of the struggle, and its all-important effect on the destiny of the race". While the editors thought it too early to describe the monument's specific character, they nonetheless agreed that the task be undertaken in the "spirit of greatness... [and] symbolise the tenacity and integrity of the British Empire; all the component races who are sharing in

---

283 Douglas Jerrold, *Georgian Adventure: The Autobiography of Douglas Jerrold* (London: The 'Right' Book Club, 1938), pp. 209-210.
284 Jay Winter, *Sites of Memory, Sites of Mourning The Great War in European Cultural History* (Cambridge: University of Cambridge Press, 1995), p. 115.

the fight must be represented".[285] Despite its patriotic and inclusive tenor, the editors cautioned that the memorial should not be the product of foolish extravagance: "We should wait until mere realism of matter and incident becomes transmuted into poetic symbols and expressions of psychologic [sic] value and ennobling effects".[286]

Although Henry T. Hare's earlier presidential address at the Royal Institute of British Architects in November 1917 remained above the fray, he peppered his remarks with both optimism and personal responsibility. A period of unprecedented opportunity awaited architects when peace returned. "Larger and broader views will be taken", Hare argued, "and it will be our duty and endeavour to ensure that such enterprises as will commemorate this critical period of our history shall be judged by generations as worthy memorials of the great events which led to their inception".[287]

It seemed for many that after four years of indescribable carnage and savage warfare the "realism of matter and incident" demanded a traditional style. The view held by the General Committee for War Memorials, formed in July 1918 at the

---

285 "Memorials of War-IV, Modern British", *The Architectural Review*, Vol. XXXVII, January-June 1915, pp. 96-104.

286 "The War Memorial Problem", *The Architectural Review*, Vol. IVII, July-December 1917, p. xviii. In June 1916, the Civic Arts Association sponsored a competition of war memorial designs commemorating the members of the London County Council staff who had been killed in the war. Held at the Royal Institute of British Architects, it offered society the chance to view differing styles, and assisted those whose job it would be to decide the tenor and tone of memorials erected after the war. A reviewer found three distinct influences: the arts and crafts movement; the "intellectual superiority" engendered by the tendencies of Rodin in sculpture; the Munich school in decorative arts and the tentacles of modern German expression in architecture; and what he labeled "the most hopeful" was the traditional. Fortunately for the reviewer, there was a "decided English flavor" to many of the works, especially to the first prize winner designed by E. A. Richards, architect, and Henry Poole, sculptor. "Civic Arts Association Competition for War Memorials", *The Architectural Review*, Vol. XL, July-December 1916, pp. 36-39.

287 Presidential Address of Henry T. Hare, *Journal of the Royal Institute of British Architects*, Vol. XXV, 5 November 1917, pp. 1-4.

Royal Academy of Art in London, reflected this dependency.

> It is essential that memorials within our churches and
> cathedrals, in the close, the public park or the village green,
> should not clash with the spirit of the past... they should
> express the emotion of the present and hope of the future
> without losing touch with the past, and that instead of
> being a rock of offense to future generations, they should
> be objects of veneration to those who follow us.[288]

The plethora of design styles raised concerns among committee
members that in perpetuating the memory of the fallen, money
would be wasted on poor designs by incompetent artists. Committee
members decided not to undertake any design responsibilities,
opting instead to limit their role to offering assistance and advice.
Despite a hands-off appearance, the committee sent a clear but
unenforceable message to municipal, institutional and philanthropic
organizations contemplating war memorials: monuments must not
clash with the spirit of the past but serve as ennobling beacons
to future generations and "the regeneration of England".[289] Any
modernist interpretations were deemed highly inappropriate.

---

288 Annual Report from the Council of the Royal Academy to the General
Assembly of Academicians for the Year 1918, pp. 69-70, Royal Academy of
Art Archives, London, England. Members of the General Committee included
the following: Sir Edward J. Poynter, Earl Ferrers, Charles Aitken, Reginald
Blomfield, Sir Thomas Brock, George Clausen, Sir Theodore Cook, Frank
Dicksee, Sir George Frampton, Henry T. Hare, C. J. Holmes W. R. Lethaby,
Rev. W. F. Norris, Sir William B. Richmond, J. S. Sargent, Charles Sims,
Sir Cecil H. Smith, Alan A. Campbell Swinton, Sir Hamo Thornycroft, Sir
Aston Webb, Christopher Whall, Henry Wilson, Captain F. Derwent Wood,
Captain H. W. Richmond and Lieutenant Colonel Sir Arthur Leetham.

289 Albert E. Richardson, "Designs for War Memorials", *Journal of the Royal
Institute of British Architects*, Vol. XXIII, 1916, pp. 287-288; William R.
Colton, "The Effects of War on Art", *The Architect & Contract Reporter*, Vol.
XCV, 17 March 1916, pp. 199-201; Memorials of War-IV, Modern British",
The Architectural Review, Vol. XXXVII, January-June 1915, pp. 96-104.

The romantic reverie of a pre-1914 Britain that helped countless individuals emerge from the scattered ashes of war and regain a sense of equilibrium proved temporary. The complex tonic of blaming the past for the present and feeling uncomfortable about the future offered scant relief. The majority of war memorials erected in village greens, schools, clubs and churches tended to be rather small and traditional, certainly not grandiose. In fact, of the 5,930 memorial unveilings, no less than 5,151 had been dedicated by 1920, and of these the majority consisted of plaques, crosses and gravestones.[290] Because the differing classes of Britain had marched together, fought together, endured privations together and died together, it seemed doubtful that traditional hierarchical structures would be restored completely. Although unmeasurable, some emotional leveling had occurred already. The government's decision to bury soldiers alongside one another regardless of rank with individual stone markers represented a tremendous departure from historical practice and a recognition of common sacrifice regardless of social class, position or rank. The Cenotaph – designed by renowned architect Edwin Lutyens – was meant originally to be a temporary structure; however, laden with visual and emotional austerity that lacked religious icons and any visible symbols celebrating victory ironically resonated with the public. One historian wrote recently that its quality was "more akin to a gasp of inarticulateness than to any congratulatory sentiment about the good that was gotten or the future that was fought for".[291] Whether purposely or accidentally, it also reflected the nascent dawn of a new democratic age.[292]

A week after the formal dedication in November 1920,

---

290 Adrian Gregory, *The Last Great War: British Society and the First World War* (Cambridge: Cambridge University Press, 2008), p. 257.

291 Allyson Booth, *Postcards from the Trenches: Negotiating the Space between Modernism & the First World War* (New York: Oxford University Press, 1996), p. 40.

292 George L. Mosse, *Fallen Soldiers: Reshaping the Memory of the World Wars* (New York: Oxford University Press, Inc., 1990), pp. 95-96.

1,250,000 people had passed silently by the memorial honouring over 700,000 soldiers who had died, leaving the base 10 feet deep in flower bouquets.[293] "The Cenotaph in Whitehall and the simple slab over the grave of the Unknown Warrior in Westminster Abbey... have taken such a hold upon the imagination of the people", H. G. Watkins stated in an address to the Birmingham Architectural Association, "it is doubtful whether any magnificent national memorial could now be erected which would make the same appeal".[294] John W. Simpson, president of the Royal Institute of British Architects, echoed similar sentiments, describing the edifice as "austere yet gracious, technically perfect... the very expression of repressed emotion, of massive simplicity of purpose, of the qualities which mark alike those whom it commemorates and those who raised it".[295] Dugald Sutherland MacColl, keeper of the Wallace Collection, Marylebone, London, offered a more solemn view. Peace had left the country bankrupt, frightfully suspicious of imagery and speeches, leaving it contented with a Cenotaph that he described as "a silence, an unseen, a nameless hero".[296]

After the memorial's formal unveiling the nation entered a labyrinthine path toward a new reality. The stealth-like tentacles of modernism – as evidenced by the admiration for the Cenotaph – were beginning to penetrate a battered, post-war society so much that it eventually had to acknowledge what it had rejected earlier. As Britain slowly emerged from its cultural depression it gradually accepted that the past *was* dead; the cultural rupture *was* complete, forcing it to face the realities of a modern world. The

---

293 Tim Skelton and Gerald Gliddon, *Lutyens and the Great War* (London: Frances Lincoln, Ltd., 2008), p. 47. Lutyens refused any payment for his work on the Cenotaph.

294 H. G. Watkins, "War Memorials", *Journal of the Royal Institute of British Architects*, Vol. XXIX, 10 February 1922, p. 284.

295 John W. Simpson, *Journal of the Royal Institute of British Architects*, Vol. XXVIII, 20 June 1921, pp. 473-474. He spoke at the presentation of the Royal Gold Medal to Sir Edwin Lutyens.

296 "Art in England", *The Morning Post*, 4-13 June 1921, p. 172.

war had obliterated the long-held belief that history and progress were intertwined. They now had become chastened. By discrediting large vestiges of the old order, the war had renewed the validity of modernisms and nurtured an environment for it to expand; however, there were consequences. Although the Great War had accelerated the pace of change and, as historian Modris Eksteins has argued, "had become the axis on which the modern world turned",[297] the war also had deprived modernisms of its youthful spirit, optimistic hopefulness and combustible energy. Modernisms now required a fresh interpretation by those who had survived yet remained damaged by the war. As *The Studio* had predicted in early 1915, new conditions would produce new results but they only would appear gradually.[298]

It became evident throughout the early 1920s that in reconstructing its material culture, society had entered a period where repulsion to modernisms – while still present – began to diminish. After the signing of the Versailles Treaty in June 1919 and the Peace Day celebrations the following month, *The Studio* believed it necessary to address the country's future in its annual *Yearbook* publication.

> Reconstruction is the popular theme of the moment and if the ideas implied by this word are carried into practice, great results will be possible in the fruitful time that is to follow the barren days of war. Many of the false trappings and superfluities of life have disappeared during four dark years. The sequence of events has cleared the way for action.[299]

---

297 Modris Eksteins, *Rites of Spring: The Great War and the Birth of the Modern Age* (Boston: Houghton Mifflin Company, 1989), p. 237.

298 "The Lay Figure: On the Art that May Be", *The Studio*, Vol. 63, 1915, p. 318.

299 Sydney R. Jones, "On the Designing of Cottages and Small Houses", *The Studio Yearbook for 1919*, pp. 1-2.

While obviously not addressing specific changes so soon after the war ended, the article's tone envisaged newness, a different way of interpreting and experiencing life. The unanswerable question remained: did reconstruction imply accepting the "new" or was it simply a desire to return to pre-1914 Britain?

One of the first noticeable differences was that the surplus wealth that had built the great country houses and the corresponding self-confidence and opulent lifestyle had evaporated with the war. "The great homes that we used to enjoy doing and seeing done by others before the war", lamented traditionalist architect Reginald Blomfield, "appear to be a thing of the past".[300] Country estates and expansive homes throughout the nation were being sold, demolished or converted into schools, care homes or other uses. In 1919 alone over a million acres had exchanged hands.[301] Society's reordering made architects realize the public demanded more from them, something that expressed the "oneness" of the British people. The editors of *The Builder* summarized that before the war the profession not only had fallen in public esteem but into disuse. Many in society had come to regard architecture either as "the frivolous business of supplying ornamentation at great cost" or "a high mystery of learning in the forms of past methods and the secrets of correct taste". Whatever the justification, it was solely for those with substantial means. "Something must be done", admonished the editors. While it agreed that some form of professional unity was required, architects needed to address the moribund state of affairs before, during and after the war. Only then could a cure for the profession's discontentedness be developed.[302]

It was with this aura of "discontentedness" in mind that soon

---

300 Reginald Blomfield, "The Exhibition of Modern British Architecture", *Journal of the Royal Institute of British Architects*, Vol. XXXIV, 7 May 1927, pp. 451-452.

301 Arthur Marwick, *The Deluge: British Society and the First World War* (Boston: Little, Brown and Company, 1965), p. 300.

302 "Our Present Discontents", *The Builder*, Vol. CXVII, 8 August 1919, p. 131.

after the July 1919 Peace Day celebrations John W. Simpson, President of the Royal Institute of British Architects, made an appeal directly to the building industry. The shortage of materials caused by war included bricks, timber and various metals, as well as the government's home building plans that invariably would cause professional architects to lose out to "generic builders" worried Simpson. Similar to what *The Builder* had published earlier, Simpson felt the public preferred generic builders because they were more affordable and less highbrow in their demeanor and approach. Invoking a bit of patriotic propaganda he drafted a memo admitting the industry's current troubles while simultaneously acknowledging a future full of promise. Britain, after all, was in a better position than most of Europe. It had defeated its "envious enemies", Simpson stated, so the only thing that remained was for everyone in the building trades "to make a strong pull, a long pull, and a pull all together, to ensure the prosperity and comfort for which we have fought".[303] He offered nothing definite and as time progressed his meager but well-intentioned effort achieved little.

Another possible remedy emerged from a deeply controversial source who was not connected to the building trade. Soon after returning from war, artist Wyndham Lewis authored a polemic titled, *The Caliph's Design: Architects, Where is Your Vortex?* (1919). It was a clarion call to architects to innovate and place themselves inside the creative vortex. Lewis believed architecture the weakest of the arts because it depended on "the collective sensibility of its period", making it more helpless and costly than painting and literature in the face of public indifference. He encouraged not only the perpetuation of modern art but its utilization in architecture – the exact fear many architects had a decade before the war. Lewis wanted to flood the "indolent commercial offices" of architects with

---

303 "Meeting of the Building Industries, Consultative Board", Special Committee Minutes, Vol. 8 – June 14, 1915-December 2, 1919, 28 August 1919, Royal Institute of British Architects Institutional Archives. Collection stored at the Victoria and Albert Museum, London.

abstract designs. "I am sure", Lewis wrote, "the result would be to cram the world with form and intention, where today… it has no discernible significance or aesthetic purpose of any sort". He knew architects of genius existed and encouraged them to emerge from their shroud of sameness. If they did, some may

> invent an architecture for our time and climate that was also a creative and fertilising art form. The first great modern building that arose in this city would soon carry everything before it; and hand in hand with the engineer and his new problems, by force of circumstances so exactly modern ones, would make a new form-content for our everyday vision. So all we want is one single architect with brains, and we will regard him with optimism.[304]

Lewis recommended that if this failed then the painter and the engineer should form a partnership. They would buy out the architect and produce neither a world of boxes nor sell antique fakes as architects had done in their "sweet and horrible way". The new partnership would banish the "stylistic architectural rubbish" of the past. Lewis encouraged using the artist even if a box or series of boxes had to be constructed. "Let us divide up this 'ramshackle Empire' of architecture", he argued.

Perhaps in an effort to gain extra credibility he quoted liberally from William R. Lethaby's handbook, *An Introduction to the History and Theory of the Art of Building*, that encouraged architects to use their historical knowledge, but not "be betrayed by it".

> The modern way of building must be flexible and vigorous, even smart and hard. We must give up designing the broken-down picturesque which is part of the ideal of make

---

304 Wyndham Lewis, *The Caliph's Design: Architects, Where is Your Vortex?* (London: The Egoist, Ltd., 1919), pp. 18-25.

believe. The enemy is not science, but vulgarity, a pretense to beauty at second hand.[305]

After applauding Lethaby's philosophy, Lewis asked, "Does not Mr. Lethaby, Professor of Architecture in the South Kensington Schools, speak to you in a tone seldom heard in the art schools? What English professor of painting would you find recommending his pupil to paint in a manner 'smart and hard'?" Lewis thought if more architects accepted Lethaby's philosophy of design, society would find "this lifeless scene had changed for the better".[306] Although Lewis had asked the difficult questions, albeit in a pseudo-confrontational manner, he never received any direct response.

Many architects disliked the publication, finding his argument superficial and lacking all semblance of reason. Lewis's detractors compared him to the ancient Athenian who always cried for the newest thing but ignored the obvious truth: "We cannot make bricks without straw". To add intensity and a bit of insult to their argument, they labeled Lewis a "Cubist", which for the time was tantamount to being called an unstable dilettante. While Lewis had described Picasso as one of the "ablest living painters", he disliked Cubism and never considered himself a progenitor or a participant in the movement. He had been a Vorticist and believed Cubism too vulnerable to whims of fashion. Moreover, concluded the architects, it was both absurd and futile for painters aided by engineers to believe they could revolutionize architecture. The Art Nouveau movement and "other schools of cranks", wrote the editors of *The Architect*, had tried years earlier to convert words and oils into deeds with disastrous results. The profession doubted whether engineers assisted by Cubist painters could solve the serious issues facing architects.

---

305 Ibid.
306 Ibid.

When they are able to prove by actual demonstration, and not barren criticism, that they can, Mr. Wyndham Lewis will be justified; till then we have a preference for criticism which is easier to understand because it is founded on facts and not on immature and hasty generalisations.[307]

Professor W. S. Purchon, Head of the Department of Architecture at Sheffield University, disagreed with his professional colleagues. He surprisingly liked the publication, believing Lewis's arguments were argued clearly and definitively. Although he considered the premise "strong meat" that may not appeal to everyone, he highly recommended it to those who had "graduated on a course of bully-beef". He compared it more to a "stimulant" and call to action rather than a "narcotic" imbued with lethargic inaction. Professor Purchon felt Lewis had grasped the issues accurately and uncovered a fundamental truth that a wiser man had missed. Purchon shared Lewis's high praise for Lethaby, affirming that his "vortex was rightly placed as well all know his heart to be".[308]

Whether John W. Simpson, president of the Royal Institute of British Architects and future architect of the British Empire Exhibition Stadium at Wembley (1924), had read Lewis's polemic is unknown, but he agreed with editors of *The Builder* that change must occur. He believed the profession was in "one of the difficult places in the age-long road of art we are building". His presidential address of November 1920 discussed the issues architects needed to work through. Simpson admitted many in society felt the work of architects the last hundred years was inferior to what had been constructed in the fourteenth or eighteenth centries or, as Simpson comically remarked, "before or after the birth of Christ". He urged

---

307 "Architectural Criticism", *The Architect*, Vol. CIII, 30 January 1920, pp. 69-70.

308 W. S. Purchon, "Review of Architects! Where is Your Vortex?", *Journal of the Royal Institute of British Architects*, Vol. XXVII, 7 February 1920, pp. 152-153.

colleagues not to despair. They had been true to the principles of the art, reminding them that if they only advanced the standard of what had gone before "by the thickness of a fingernail" they would rank with the great masters of all time. Criticism of architecture, Simpson argued, arose because of the increasingly poor quality of contemporary art whose mantra was to

> break away altogether from the past, to find a new and short road to aesthetic expression. Exasperated by incessant taunts, unbalanced minds are stampeded from the quiet fields of honest study into the frantic eccentricities which, now and again, astonish us – and vanish into oblivion.

Despite the tentativeness of modern culture Simpson felt the profession was on the cusp of a new departure. He compared the recent technological advancements in warfare to what was in the offing for architecture. The machine age had arrived and the profession needed to adapt. There was no incongruity between machine work and architecture but there was nothing more incongruous than reviving medieval artistry in the twentieth century. Simpson also offered colleagues important advice. He encouraged them to take a wider view of what constituted "tradition", shed deep-seated prejudices, and find innovative ways to address contemporary needs. Known as a man who appreciated "the ideas, aims and work of architects in other lands", Simpson thought it wasteful to pine incessantly about past traditions.[309] "Our problems are altered", Simpson concluded, "and we have to solve them in our own way". He thought if buildings were designed and constructed for contemporary purposes then the artistic/ aesthetic component would be taken care of organically.[310] Although colleagues may not have acted on all suggestions immediately, his

---

309 "Obituary", *Journal of the Royal Institute of British Architects*, Vol. XV, April 1933, pp. 514-515, 557.

310 John W. Simpson, "Inaugural Address", *Journal of the Royal Institute of British Architects*, Vol. XXVII, 6 November 1920, pp. 1-9.

comments served as a directional beacon toward a new paradigm that some architects embraced as the decade progressed. Perhaps more importantly, discussions surrounding design modernisms since the war had become less infused with emotion and more reliant on intellect. Whether the promoters or the detractors of modernisms recognized it, their respective arguments acknowledged the reality of a changed world.

The war had discredited history and in its wake a different society had emerged. Architects began to understand that if they wanted to obtain the support of those who won the war they no longer could design edifices reminiscent of the Middle Ages, or Georgian or Victorian eras. Such structures seemed highly inappropriate. To continue this course was tantamount either to mocking or to ignoring the needs of contemporary life. One architect argued that while the profession needed to learn from and perpetuate tradition, it was equally important to understand what to discard. "The *true* is usually overlaid with much error", he wrote, "and the winnowing process is difficult". Nevertheless, he admitted that a properly designed structure from the past – one that had stood the test of time – actually housed within it the very seeds for the future.[311] As a living art, architecture could no longer be dependent on the past. The war, in fact, had made extensive portions of the past irrelevant. Conditions had changed. Symbolisms were different. The public desired original designs that were sympathetic to contemporary times, not the reflections of past ages. Architects who understood history slowly began to appreciate that when an experimental innovation succeeded, it usually indicated the concepts established by previous traditions had loosened or partially broken down. True professionals would not deliberately abandon working within the prescribed limits of existing formulae unless they were no longer applicable.

---

311 William E. Sanders, "Modernism and Design", *The Builder*, Vol. CXII, 13 January 1922, p. 69.

Architect Howard Robertson, soon to be involved in designing the British Pavilion for the 1925 Paris Exposition, expressed a similar opinion to colleagues at the Birmingham Architectural Association. He believed architects had not only failed to benefit by the heritage of tradition, they had not added to it. Perhaps "its grandeur had intimidated them", Robertson suggested, "[or] because they had depended upon it instead of attempting by original thought to make tradition themselves".[312] Because architecture both crystallized the propensity of the age and expressed the culture of an entire generation, a few post-war architects appreciated the changed dynamic and slowly abandoned the quest for a new architecture that imposed the past upon contemporary life. They endeavored to create designs sympathetic to current conditions and to the demands of a new world. This task of restoring the structural art of architecture to its proud heritage that benefited from tradition yet added to it proved difficult. It involved breaking one tradition to make way for another.

Other opinions resurrected the democratic philosophy expressed before the war that encouraged architects to consider the prejudices and realities of modern society. A host of new problems had materialized in post-war Britain: the "economic rent" issue, the "new rich" and the "new poor" issue, the domestic servant problem and, of course, low industrial wages. An increased level of democracy already had occurred in some areas, from representation in town councils to limited women enfranchisement. Some social leveling had seeped into the public's expectations of what kind of architecture homes and cities should reflect, including what welfare amenities would provide a healthy and comfortable environment. "The men who held the Hun at Ypres and threw him back from the Marne", wrote an anonymous architect, "have lived in just those dreary surroundings that are the feature of the East End of

---

312 Howard Robertson, "Modernism in Architecture", *The Builder*, Vol. CXXVII, 3 October 1924, p. 524.

our big cities". Architects owed them a great deal and would be indispensable in ensuring the country they fought to save was worth living in. "The war has accustomed us to a grander scale of ideas", continued the writer, "a fuller conception of our power as a united nation and the community will now demand an expression of this in some permanent form".[313] The post-war environment afforded architects opportunities to contribute to a diverse clientele with contemporary needs. Whether architects heeded the advice and fulfilled society's expectations remains problematic and open to debate. To more independently inclined architects, however, the post-war era had loosened the obligation to unflinchingly follow tradition. Enough debate and discussion had occurred the past decade to permit the more adventuresome to explore modernisms' potential. Although lacking a firm commitment from the profession, it appeared that new architecture could be studied and, if found appropriate, utilized.

Roger Fry re-entered the discussion in early 1921 when the Royal Institute of British Architects sponsored a lecture series designed to arouse public interest in architecture. Interestingly Fry's involvement may have been piqued by Wyndham Lewis's controversial work *The Caliph's Design: Architects, Where is Your Vortex?* published two years earlier. The two head-strong artists had worked closely together at The Omega Workshops managed by Fry prior to the Great War but parted company acrimoniously in late 1913 due to a badly handled artistic commission. The two men never reconciled. While Fry showed genuine interest and concern in the state of architecture, his public address could be interpreted as a tactic ensuring Lewis was not the only Bloomsbury voice heard in the debate.

Fry titled his presentation "Architectural Heresies of a Painter". He identified several causes for the lamentable condition of British

---

313 A. Layman, "Architects and the Future of England", *The Builder*, Vol. CXVI, 3 January 1919, p. 10.

architecture. The most obvious problem was the "art of architecture" had been replaced by the "art of dressing buildings" according to current fashion. Typically the designs obtained a brief air of curious novelty only to become passé a few years later. Even Britain's sole architectural accolade could not be celebrated: it excelled at designing buildings with an incredibly poor sense of proportion and scale. Fry identified Portland Place as the only commercial/residential area in London where one could, as he termed it, "spread the wings of one's civic consciousness". While he admitted that occasionally structures of good taste emerged, they inevitably were private buildings and not official or public buildings. And by good taste Fry meant social good taste – by not being dowdy, slack or unscholarly. He found most buildings lacked any semblance of aesthetic virtue because they became too dependent on recreating the social-historical elements of the past. While all structures were three-dimensional, most suffered from not having a three-dimensional form where all constituent shapes and elements were thought about and planned in advance by architects possessing vivid imaginations, and were not merely the results of accident or necessity. This failing existed because most architects, according to Fry, unfortunately "thought and felt in the flat". Similar to other aspects of Britain's cultural life, he believed social snobbery seemed at the root of most architecture. Contemporary conditions and scientific-engineering had provided the greatest opportunity for architects in history but their feeble attempts were found wanting. They lacked the experimental *elan* that would have made their designs inspirational. Fry tried not to be too harsh, arguing the vices that architecture exhibited were not new but had been present throughout most of the nation's history. Modern conditions only exacerbated the problem. This failure was not solely the fault of architects. Fry understood many defects emanated from inherited custom and over time had become thoroughly inculcated. Only by confronting these issues directly, Fry argued, could the first steps be taken toward improvement: "It was just the advantage of our highly self-conscious and critical age that we could by a deliberate effort change our character". Fry apologized that the list appeared horridly abrupt and perhaps a bit coarse but he failed to see any way of taking out its painful sting.[314]

In a follow-up interview with *The Times* a few days later Fry admitted the difficulty in trying to solve Britain's architecture problem. He spoke out merely to make the public more aware of the issue. Excessive use of ornament had ruined architecture during the past two hundred years, producing structures of limited worth. And its continued use had become so predictable that by the time the war began, ubiquitous ornamentation had almost become the rule. "The war has abolished a good deal of ornament from our lives", Fry argued, "and at least, through economic causes, it is weeding ornament out of architecture". Fry found it ironic that the quality of the country's architecture had diminished for two hundred years yet might be uplifted and improved due to economic constraints. In fact, Fry confessed that post-war designs were not as bad as some that had gone before. Although he did not name a specific building, he reiterated that the war's aftermath with the scarcity of resources and relative costliness had caused a slight improvement. When asked what recently constructed building suited his idea of excellence, Fry replied the Kodak Building on the Kingsway, London. He thought the construction arose largely from its materials that sprang naturally from its means. If Fry had his way, he would have developed it even further. "If buildings or objects only carry out what they intend in the best possible way, they are naturally beautiful". Perhaps, Fry concluded, the unsettled economy might offer architects the opportunity to reintroduce natural beauty so that aesthetic beauty reappears.[315]

The ever-stalwart Reginald Blomfield responded immediately and quite aggressively to Fry's comments. He and many colleagues

---

314 Roger Fry, "Architectural Heresies of a Painter", *Journal of the Royal Institute of British Architects*, Vol. XXVIII, 19 May 1921, pp. 436-437.

315 "Ugly Buildings. Mr. Fry on Useless Ornament", *The Times*, 23 May 1921, p. 7.

considered Fry an artistic rebel whose views reflected those of a "visionary" instead of a practical architect. Blomfield admitted the disastrous use of irrelevant ornamentation in the past but that had been rectified. He also felt architects had understood for years that the true beauty of a structure was found in efficiency and expression of purpose. The problem with modern buildings constructed after the war was builders and not architects had designed the structures. This arrangement increased exponentially after the government launched its "Homes for Heroes" legislation. Architecture was an art form, Blomfield emphasized, but recently – within the last decade or so – it had become a professional business. Architecture needed to return to its artistic foundation. Unlike Fry, Blomfield failed to find any merit in the Kodak Building. "To my mind", he lamented, "it is not even what Mr. Fry would call 'tolerable'".[316]

Architects who envisaged modern designs looked toward Europe with interest but not necessarily with great enthusiasm. Lengthy articles appeared regularly in professional trade journals highlighting modern trends throughout Scandinavia, France, Hungary, Germany, Austria and the Netherlands, a feature that had figured prominently in several publications before the war.[317] The images depicted what some referred to as "the modern madness" of European designs, enabling many to draw an architectural parallel to the work of Cubist painters. Others drew a political comparison and went as far as to suggest modernism simply was "architectural Bolshevism".[318] Less reactionary architects, however, remained flummoxed whether such bold experimentation had longevity, could be adapted to Britain and, as they had before the outbreak of war, became concerned

---

316 "Ugly Buildings. Sir R. Blomfield and Mr. Fry", *The Times*, 24 May 1921, p. 13.
317 "Architectural Madness", *The Architect*, Vol. CVIII, 29 September 1922, pp. 215-216; Howard Robertson, "Modern Dutch Architecture", *The Architectural Review*, Vol. LIV, July-December 1923, pp. 97-101; "Stylism or Nihilism in Architecture?" *The Architect*, Vol. CXII, 31 October 1924, pp. 266-267.
318 "Architectural Madness", *The Architect*, Vol. CVIII, 29 September 1922, pp. 215-216.

whether it was possible to invent new forms. While the goal of a British architecture unencumbered by foreign influences remained important, it seemed that after coming under constant assault the mantra had begun to lose its pre-war imperial intensity.

In 1924, the editors of *The Architect* reviewed recent designs in Germany, perhaps as a harbinger of what Britain soon might experience. In a somewhat pompous manner they dismissed Erich Mendelsohn's design of the Weichmann Silkstore manufacturing facility and offices in Gleiwitz, Upper Silesia, as yet another of the "new expression" edifices based on

> the treatment of a building as a square block broken by ranges of windows arranged to emphasize horizontal lines and with massive horizontal concrete projections here and there to still further emphasize horizontal proportions. The grouping of windows at an angle, a structural difficulty with most materials, but a feat easily compassed when ferro-concrete is the material used, and the use of a certain proportion of rough brickwork to give variety, seems to cover the whole of the range of Mendelsohnian compositions which are singular without affording any evidence of suggested newer basis of architectural forms.

Britain's architects had designed similar buildings with more simplified details, the editors argued, but conspicuously had avoided the "noticed exaggeration" which Mendelsohn had carried to "absurd length", including the structure's overall horizontal articulation as well as a flat roof. While the editors thought it an easy task to design a building similar to Mendelsohn, they quickly dismissed the idea, arguing it would be a style "we should tire of with constant repetition… " Furthermore, configuring concrete into horizontal shapes and linear angles only constituted a revelation in architectural style if the same design could not have been completed using other materials. It only would have significance, wrote *The Architect*, if concrete was the sole material capable of creating a truly revolutionary design.[319] The editors failed unfortunately to appreciate the tremendous changes Mendelsohn's architectural designs had undergone since the completion in 1921 of the Expressionist-styled Einstein Tower on Telegraphenberg Hill in Potsdam, Germany, a unique structure that had been derived from his war experience.

Whatever professional or philosophical arguments opponents used to combat modernism, the majority, except the most stalwart and determined, seemed resigned to the inevitable: Continental modernisms would crystalize and eventually influence British architecture. Such semi-despondency only heightened the widespread trepidation that the denationalization of architecture would lead to an internationalist style shared by all nations yet owned by none. More disconcerting, however, was that such designs eventually would prevent any chance for a purely British design erected on British soil. The realization that the long sought after initiative to create the definitive British architecture probably would not be fulfilled proved difficult to accept.

The inconceivability that the past lacked relevancy meant cutting-edge modernisms made little direct headway in the early 1920s. Britain remained a country where tradition died hard, if it died at all. The country's highly admired conservative bias, prone to overdo its zealousness in protecting British architectural traditions, could not accept the past was dead and instead continued to embrace tradition in preference to experimentation. Attempting to create something new from what opponents defined as "the lowest common multiple of all people's characteristics" would never flourish in architecture.[320] Although some British architects constantly analyzed how to approach modernism and tried in vain to understand it – to see if *any* portion

---

319 "Stylism or Nihilism in Architecture?", *The Architect*, Vol. CXII, 31 October 1924, pp. 266-267.
320 "Art and Internationalism", *The Architectural Review*, Vol. LX, July-December 1926, p. 50.

would be appropriate for Britain – the security of tradition buttressed by history remained an impregnable barrier. Soon, however, web-like cracks began to surface.

In addition to the tremendous economic dislocation experienced after the war – rapid inflation, lower wages, rising unemployment, housing shortages, industrial unrest including miners, railway workers and police strikes, as well as the diminution of world trade – a price also was paid for the residual effects of the jingoistic rants and poisonous diatribes that had motivated civilized nations to fight a war that resulted in a "butcher bill" or casualty list totaling into the millions. "It seems likely", wrote a British historian, "that public life at all levels suffered a deterioration of standards and a decline of taste".[321] The horribleness of the war provided the perfect excuse for many in society to ignore convention and free themselves from expectations. The war became an apology for the way they led their life. How could society question their unorthodox behavior when the nation had endured the prodigiousness of world war? As a result, British artists in the early 1920s seemed unable to make their works resonate with a disinterested public. The artists too, for that matter, found themselves at a creative crossroads. Their ability to wage dissent or assert independent values as they had done prior to the war proved unusually challenging. Many modern artists succumbed either by choice or by accident to the stalled, post-war culture and in softening their approach accurately depicted society's directionless drift.

Walter H. Godfrey, architect, avid building conservationist and architectural historian, bemoaned the disruptive condition of post-war British art. The lack of a national art consciousness had created a plethora of modern styles, he thought, which accurately reflected the disquiet of the times.

---

321 David Thomson, *England in the Twentieth Century* (London: Jonathan Cape, 1964).

The artist is no subtle thinker; not adept at self-analysis; he is seeking the means of expression, directly, emotionally and he needs a full diet which the present day denies him. In a state of semi-starvation his emotions fly to the works of every and any master for the nutriment which the life of his fellows cannot afford him; but since he can seldom reason safely about his work or his environment, he imagines that each of his quests is a reflection of a genuinely modern aim. He is right only in so far as the diversity of his own and his brother artist's ambitions reflects the uncertainty of current convictions and the absence of an articulate purpose in society.

Godfrey predicted that it would be a well-trodden road before a coordinated style – where "we shall see the threads worked into the one great woven tapestry" – could represent the present age. Despite sounding pessimistic he nevertheless believed the days of the Philistine well-fortified in an entrenched camp were numbered, for the purifying influence of the war would take effect soon. "Entry has been made into so many of his strongholds that he has already been forced out into the open", Godfrey argued, "and is becoming somewhat ashamed of his nakedness". He admitted that some new art was beautiful and held great promise for the future but would infiltrate and then dominate only when "our hearts have learned to beat in time".[322] That day and time, concluded Godfrey, could not be predicted.

A sliver of brightness gradually illuminated a barely visible horizon. After a five-year absence, Britain's interest in modern French art reappeared in August 1919 with the *Exhibition of Modern French Art* at Heal's Mansard Gallery housed within the newly opened and modernly designed Heal & Sons, Ltd. store

---

322 Walter H. Godfrey, "Some Examples of Modern Memorials – I", *The Architectural Review*, Vol. XLVII, January-June 1920, pp. 13-16.

on London's Tottenham Court Road.[323] Curated by Osbert and Sacheverell Sitwell, it included works by Matisse, Picasso, Derain, Survage, Soutine, Leger and several others. The exhibition demonstrated that French art not only had remained vital but more importantly, the war had not killed the modern movement. "There is stir and effort and experiment", Clive Bell wrote, "within the movement there is a lively reaction: there is a *juenesse*".[324] It was also the first time the public experienced works by Amedeo Modigliani and, as Osbert Sitwell recalled a bit disappointingly, some of their reactions proved that despite the war Britain remained a nation of "Philistines in Arms".[325] One patron, Greville MacDonald, M.D., wrote to the *Nation* complaining that on one level the whole collection seemed nothing but a glorification of prostitution and on another

> ... I felt it must be an attempt to prove that all revolution however necessary for the redemption of society or morality or art, has only one ending – that of sans-culottism: and that, meaning less the exchange of court-breeches for plebeian trousers, than the discarding of every convention of decency.[326]

His reaction started a cavalcade of letters to the *Nation*. Many supported MacDonald's comments, while others defended the exhibition's content. Bell pitied MacDonald, believing he and his supporters should accept that the battle was over. They had lost.

---

323 An advertisement for "Heal's New Shop" called the structure a "distinguished... piece of modern architecture". *The Times*, 17 May 1917, p. 8. Designed by Dunbar Smith and Cecil Brewer, the building offered what Alan Powers described as a "dignified and rational street architecture without self-conscious 'period' detail". Alan Powers, *Britain: Modern Architecture in History* (London: Reaktion Books, Ltd., 2007), p. 25.

324 Osbert Sitwell, *Laughter in the Next Room* (London: The Reprint Society, 1949), p. 325.

325 Ibid, p. 149.

326 Ibid, pp. 328-330.

The world was very different now. Bell referenced that even *The Times* recognized modern art had triumphed by highlighting a special French supplement in the 6 September issue detailing the movement's young masters. MacDonald and his ilk were the "gallant defenders of a lost cause", Bell admonished. "As such they are entitled to our affectionate esteem, for which, however, they are not likely to thank us".[327]

The Canadian War Memorial Exhibition held during the winter of 1919 at the Royal Academy, Burlington House, London, offered the public a comprehensive and eclectic depiction of the war, from the front lines of combat to the banal activities occurring in the rear. Commissioned by the Ministry of Information and the Canadian Government, it contained 400 paintings by both men and women from Canada and several other nations. Some canvases would never have been sanctioned let alone displayed publicly a few years earlier, leading the *Daily Express* to declare that both the Canadians and the Royal Academy had let many "Rebels in the Fortress".[328] The public surprisingly accepted the modernist interpretations without being overwhelmed by them. This irony was not lost on the critics. *The Times* labeled the exhibit "Art's Fresh Start". The war "has supplied a momentous theme, while it is an event in itself so large, and so shattering of continuity, that even the dullest of us expect all things to be different after it".[329] Works displayed included: John Singer Sargent's *Gassed*, Paul Nash's *The Menin Road*, Stanley Spencer's *Travoys*, William Robert's *A Shell Dump*, Anna Airy's *Cook House at Witley Camp,* David Young Cameron's *The Battlefield of Ypres*, George Clausen's *The Gun Factory at Woolwich Arsenal 1918*, Laura Knight's *Physical Training (Boxing) Witley Camp*, C. R. W. Nevinson's *War in the Air* and Wyndham Lewis's *Canadian Gun Pit*. Although the editors of *The Architect* described it as the most

---

327 Ibid, pp. 338-339.

328 *Daily Express*, 3 January 1919.

329 "Art's Fresh Start. A War Revolution. Experiences in Paint", *The Times*, 12 December 1919, p. 15.

remarkable exhibition held in years, especially for the normally staid Royal Academy, they nonetheless found it disruptive.

> Tradition is often ignored, and we are presented with a group of pictures which suggests a standard of painting largely incomprehensible we daresay to the majority of visitors to the exhibition. It is a standard of art which, broadly, does not explain itself, but which requires that the spectator should resolve what was in the mind of the artist when he painted the picture, what his intention was, and how far he has carried out his intention.[330]

The exhibition was a definite reaction against academic art, allowing the editors to exclaim emphatically but somewhat awkwardly: "We find no joy in them; we like them not". They acknowledged that in certain periods of history a reaction against accepted standards might indicate a level of "health and vitality" – and that may well be what was occurring at the Royal Academy – but it all seemed too "incomprehensible" for the present.[331] The *Nation* echoed similar sentiments: "More than ten million people, mainly men, have died violent deaths in Europe. Why? It is no use going to Burlington House to find out".[332] At a time when the works may have helped society understand the hell of combat and accept the art created by soldier-artists who experienced war and painted it, there remained a nagging sense of the paintings' disquietude.

By the early 1920s, artists, critics and the public, perhaps echoing Walter Godfrey's earlier sentiments, believed for a multitude of conflicting reasons a malady had descended upon contemporary British art. William George Constable, art historian, art curator and the first director of the Courtauld Institute of Art in 1931, believed

---

330 "The Nation's War Paintings at the Royal Academy", *The Architect*, Vol. CIII, 2 January 1920, p. 10.

331 Ibid.

332 "The Picture of the Sphinx", *Nation*, 28 January 1919.

art was in a "lamentable state" and would not progress until it had regained its "lost traditions and recover[ed] some *elan vitale*". He felt the most meaningful way to accomplish this was to make the public aware of the best art, especially modern art, because it was "more directly a function of modern life than the art of the past can ever be, and is therefore more likely to awaken response from its contemporaries". Although Constable lavished praise on modern art he did not ignore the past. He confessed that merely to imitate past work was foolish, but to disregard it was even worse. Similar to what traditionalist-leaning architects had advocated for decades, Constable encouraged artists to use the past wisely because "discoveries and conquests of the past become the stepping stones to advance and inspiration founded on modern experiences… "[333]

Despite extreme differences among members and patrons of the Royal Academy, the New English Art Club and the London Group or the acolytes of Cubist and Futurist styles, all shared a similar belief: more was wrong with British art than right. Many thought it was in a chronic, invalid state.[334] One critic predicted a hundred years would have to pass before anyone would realize what the "aesthetic sects were really aiming at… [because] most of us are wandering in the dark without being able to find such a key".[335] Others, however, felt confident that although void of academic propriety and conventional subject matter, new art reflected spontaneity and the adventurous spirt of youth that ultimately would triumph.[336]

In an effort to find a compromise between these opposing views and to elevate the importance of fine art in Britain's post-

---

333 William G. Constable, "Modern Art at the Victoria Art Gallery, Bath", *Burlington Magazine*, Vol. XXXVI, February 1920, pp. 88-89.

334 "Modern British Painting – A Proposal", *Burlington Magazine*, Vol. XXXVIII, April 1921, pp. 155-156. Clive Bell made this comment in the March 1921 issue of *Burlington Magazine*.

335 "Mr. Nevinson's Work", *The Architect*, Vol. CXI, 21 March 1924, p. 194.

336 "A New Direction in Art", *The Builder*, Vol. CXXI, 7 October 1921, p. 436.

war culture, the editors of *Burlington Magazine* created the *Nameless Exhibition of Paintings and Drawings by Contemporary British Artists*. Additional goals included lifting the veil of ignorance and invigorating a fresh interest in contemporary painting, ridding society of its "cantankerous prejudices", and improving the way artists conveyed art to the public. Held at the Grosvenor Galleries on Bond Street, London, from 20 May-2 July 1921, and curated by three judges of dissimilar artistic tastes, the exhibition displayed 171 works by 97 artists – from the academic and classical traditionalism of the Royal Academy to the contemporary modernist works. Works displayed included *Kitty of Frying Pan Alley* by Oswald Birley, *Portrait of Philip Wilson Steer* and *Brighton Pierrots,* both by Walter Sickert, *Christ Carrying the Cross* by Stanley Spencer, *Study after 'The Lemon Gatherers'* by Duncan Grant, *Strolling Players* by Henry Tonks and *Portrait of Iris Tree Seated on a Four-Poster Bed* by Alvaro Guevara. A unique feature of the exhibition was the artwork remained unidentified when displayed and in the catalogue listing. The respective artist's name was revealed only toward the end of the exhibition's six-week run.

The experiment proved successful, instructive and inherently controversial. Instead of serving as a breeding ground for snobbery and personal prejudices as had been feared, the editors of *Burlington Magazine* – perhaps a bit self-serving – believed it offered "the best stimulus imaginable to that critical sense which lies dormant or servile in most of us".[337] More importantly perhaps the exhibition encouraged a sympathetic and acceptable attitude toward modern art and served as a primer for Britain as it continued toward developing a new reality less dependent on the past. Art historians today believe it should be viewed in the context of its time, as

---

337 "Modern British Painting – A Proposal", *Burlington Magazine*, Vol. XXXVIII, April 1921, pp. 155-156; Desmond MacCarthy, "The Nameless Exhibition", *Burlington Magazine*, Vol. XXXVIII, June 1921, pp. 261-262. The judges included Roger Fry, fine art organizer and critic; Henry Tonks, painter and professor of art at the Slade School of Art; and Charles Sims of the Royal Academy.

"consolidating and building on the achievements of the pre-War years, and… [be considered as] a logical successor to Fry's Post Impressionist exhibitions of 1910 and 1912".[338]

Some contemporary critics withheld support. *The Architectural Review* thought the whole idea ridiculous and displaying canvases without the artist's name absurd.

> We are threatened with an art exhibition at which the names of the artists will not be revealed until the show is nearly over. The idea is to evade the magic of personality – to bring the public and the artists to see these pictures with eyes unjaded by the accumulated memories of many shows, by the battalion of artists' surnames, the nomenclature of schools. It is a futile notion. An experienced critic is not at all likely to be baffled by the mere absence of names… For him the painter signs his work – not with a name, but with a method that is as peculiar to him as his finger-prints.[339]

The fear of democratization, that the public might be capable of comparing and contrasting artworks without the assistance of professional critics, proved powerfully strong. *The Builder* was afraid it might not go far enough to break down barriers. It encouraged curators to venture outward into new directions, beyond official sources, groups and schools, where some of the most vital art was being created.[340] Despite these reservations, the exhibition's wider importance was it helped society realize that although void of academic propriety and sometimes emotionally immature, new art was in the ascendant, accurately interpreting contemporary life while simultaneously capturing the adventurous spirit of the

---

338 Samuel Elmer, "Nameless Exhibition, London, 1921", *Burlington Magazine*, Vol. CLIII, September 2011, pp. 583-590.

339 "Anonymous Art", *The Architectural Review*, Vol. 49, p. xxxii.

340 "Nameless Art", *The Builder*, Vol. CXX, 15 April 1921, p. 464.

modern age.[341] In many instances the quality of new art surpassed academic or traditional art. As the critic for the *Daily News* argued, the exhibition "will teach the onlooker, if he is candid with himself, a great deal about the limits of his own knowledge".[342]

Great change also was afoot by those who acquired artwork for the national galleries. In 1924, Samuel Courtauld established a £50,000 trust fund for the Tate Gallery to acquire Impressionist and Post-Impressionist artworks. The fact that the same institution had turned down the gift of a Degas a mere twenty years earlier demonstrated that a significant, almost seismic, shift had occurred. *The Contemporary Review* put it all in perspective. In 1910, Roger Fry had let Britain view and laugh at works by Cézanne, Van Gogh and Gauguin but now "we are all converted".

> Though our new enthusiasm somewhat resembles the fervour of a revivalist meeting and our applause is a little uncritical, still our conversion has done us good; it has opened our insular eyes and set us thinking furiously... One day, when we all know them better and the mist of incense is dispelled, we shall be able to judge them more acutely, and with that knowledge will come an infinitely greater appreciation of their work.

It would have been a shock, the critic continued, if Britain had not discovered that "a great movement had been born, had flourished and had died almost under our very eyes [which] has made us feel ashamed of not having known about it all a little sooner".[343] The real misfortune, however, was the relative ease with which an insular nation had turned away so determinately from artistic developments on the Continent earlier in the century.

---

341 "A New Direction in Art", and "Art and a New Age," *The Builder*, Vol. CXXI, 7 October 1921, pp. 436-437.

342 *Daily News*, 19 May 1921, p. 5.

343 W. A. Propert, "The Courtauld Gift to the National Gallery", *The Contemporary Review*, Vol. 125, January 1924, pp. 72-77.

The critic offered the trustees unsolicited advice not to squander the acquisition money. Purchases should only be the best examples of French modern art. Second-rate works took up space and eventually would be deaccessioned. Such patience, the critic emphasized, will earn the trustees the public's gratitude and dispel the notion that the committee was incapable of understanding modern art.[344]

Immediate and more serious post-war issues prevented the government from creating the Ministry of Fine Arts as had been proposed a few weeks before the war declaration. By 1924, however, political leaders finally sensed the need to act and put their weight and considerable influence behind establishing the Royal Fine Arts Commission. Although falling below the level of a cabinet ministry as had been hoped originally, its membership remained distinguished: David Alexander Edward Lindsay – 27th Earl of Crawford and 10th Earl of Balcarres, George Nathanial Curzon – Lord Curzon of Kedleston, Aston Webb, Reginald Blomfield, Edwin Lutyens, Alfred Gotch, George Frampton, David Y. Cameron and Thomas H. Mawson. The Commission lacked regulatory authority, but Parliament and local councils as well as private organizations who desired assistance on artistic, aesthetic and design matters sought its considered opinion. *The Architect* hoped the body would prove useful and not hesitate to use its power to discourage attempts to erect war memorials that lacked "inadequate funds and inadequate scope".[345] While neither outwardly progressive nor stodgily conservative, it certainly leaned toward quelling the outlandish tendencies architects and artists may have had in appealing to a more democratic, post-war audience. Members reviewed a number of different issues during monthly meetings. Topics discussed in the Commission's formative years included new post box design, extensions to government buildings, design of public memorials, preserving or replacing the existing Waterloo Bridge, the placement

344 Ibid.
345 "Fine Art Commission", *The Architect*, 1 February 1924, p. 76.

of General Earl Haig's statue near the Cenotaph, a new entrance to University College London, artistic murals for the new Foreign Gallery at the Tate, and redecorating the Foreign Office's reception rooms.[346]

As the cultural pendulum continued to swing, obtaining acceptance of new art and new architecture also included broadening education. In 1925, art critic Frank Rutter, architect Cyril Power and artist Claude Flight formed the Grosvenor School of Modern Art located at 33 Warwick Square, Pimlico, London. Besides possessing abundant enthusiasm, the three men were well qualified to found a new educational/artistic institution. Rutter was an art critic for *The Sunday Times*, an early supporter of modern art in Britain and founder of the Allied Artists Association. Power was an artist and architect who lectured on architectural design and history at the School of Architecture, University College London. Flight was an artist known for linocut prints and wood cuts who, in 1923, had joined the newly formed Seven and Five Society whose members included artists Henry Moore and Barbara Hepworth. *The Architect* proudly announced the school's opening to readers: "New School of Modern Art for Architects and Others". The school offered general lectures and practical instruction on the modern ideas of art including special classes for architects. While it became famous for printmaking and developing cutting-edge linocutting techniques in a distinctive Futurist style, it made a concerted effort to provide architects with a solid grounding in art history with special emphasis on modern art movements.[347]

---

346 Records of the Royal Fine Arts Commission, Minutes, 1924-1929, BP 1/1 and BP 1/2, National Archives, London. The professional journal *The Architect* thought such an organization was too bureaucratic. "Those whose work lies in the direction of the arts", the editors wrote, "can best serve those interests by achievement rather than by propaganda". "Art in Common Life," *The Architect*, Vol. CV, 1 April 1921, pp. 219-220.

347 "New School of Modern Art for Architects and Others", *The Architect*, Vol. CXIV, 3 October 1925, p. 308. The school operated until 1940.

All these events surrounding modern art, from exhibitions and museum acquisitions to education and government oversight committees, demonstrated how far general acceptance had come since the country's first exposure in 1905 to the "new". This slow, meandering and indeed controversial process should not be interpreted as merely a transition. It amounted to much more. While the war certainly did not create modernisms, the war did cause a fundamental shift in the way Britain perceived its cultural reality. Post-war life had become detached from pre-war life. There could be no going back. Society had reached a point of no return. The continuity with the past that so many had taken for granted before 1914 had been severed permanently by 1925. In late 1927, the editors of *The Builder* struck a reflective cord that pithily described the nation's state of affairs.

> After the chaos which is the aftermath of war, we are slowly emerging into what seems to be very largely a new world. Changes which in the normal course of things would have taken a generation to accomplish, have been greatly accelerated, and have come abruptly upon us in a few years. We are faced with new ideas, new conditions, new materials and new requirements.[348]

Even the most conservative in society came to realization that the past had to be left behind, eventually accepting the uncomfortableness of a new taxonomy of reality.

By 1924-1925, many architects underwent a subtle but important philosophical change: for British architecture to survive and to prosper its practitioners needed to leave the isolated *ateliers* and mingle with their fellow citizens. Some understood that for their own advancement they needed to eliminate prejudices against

---

348 "Architectural Expression", *The Builder*, Vol. CXXXIII, 25 November 1927, p. 803.

experiment and study the modernistic successes of other countries. Moreover, they needed to design and not copy, abandon the preponderance of historical Greco-Roman inspired designs, and discard the trappings of historical consciousness. Some understood that if a structure's purpose embodied dignity, truth and simplicity at the expense of meretricious detail, a more harmonious orderliness would result.[349] It was essential to overcome what progressive architect Howard Robertson identified as their "sluggish repression" toward the modern and relinquish any inclination to apply methods used earlier.[350] James O'Hanlon Hughes, a well-known architect of churches, a published poet and informed student of history, urged colleagues to prepare themselves. He compared architects to authors and poets, believing they too must study life first-hand and interpret their own age for posterity even though that message consisted of natural stone.

> Our problems in life and art are 'our' problems, and in an age of doubt and perplexity the platitudes of a tranquil past are sounding rather hollow. But we are still in their thrall, and the grip of their ancient tyranny lies heavy on our souls. Only by a courageous effort to think for ourselves the solution of our own perplexing problems can be progress, and the craftsmen look to us as the true and natural leaders, and the age awakens to inspiration of our work.[351]

His prescriptive advice reflected the war's impact on how society was grappling with the "platitudes of a tranquil past". While difficult

---

349 F. Ernest Crutchley, "Letter to the Editor", *The Builder*, Vol. CXXXVI, 28 March 1924, p. 488.

350 "Modernism in Architecture", *The Builder*, Vol. CXXVII, 3 October 1924, p. 524; "How Difficult it is to Keep Modern", *The Architect*, Vol. CXIII, 6 February 1925, p. 99.

351 James O'Hanlon Hughes, "The Young Architects & The Humanities", *The Builder*, Vol. CXXIII, 27 March 1925, p. 481.

and perhaps painful to accept, architects needed to grasp the realization that the 17ᵗʰ, 18ᵗʰ or 19ᵗʰ century provided few answers to 20ᵗʰ century queries about architectural design.

The completion of Adelaide House in 1925, located on King William Street at London Bridge, signified a new beginning for architecture. Many recognized John James Burnet's structure almost immediately as an immense stepping-stone toward progress that borrowed little from the past. *The Times* proudly described it as "A Turning-Point in London". Sir John James Burnet's career had been laden with successes. He had served as president of the Glasgow Institute of Architects and designed buildings and memorials including the eponymous Kodak Building (1910-1911) on Kingsway, London, the Edward VII Gallery extension to the British Museum (1905), Selfridge's Department Store expansion, London (1919) and war memorials located in Palestine, Suez and Gallipoli (1919) to name a few. Burnet was knighted in 1914 in acknowledgement of his well-received addition to the British Museum.

Adelaide House embodied the ideas he and other progressive architects had been discussing since the war ended: combining design and function into one homogeneous expression.[352] Perhaps most importantly it served as the foundation for Britain accepting a new tradition by being quintessentially "modern". Architect Howard Robertson, himself in the deepening throes of designing the British Pavilion for the 1925 *Exposition des Arts Decoratifs et Industriels Modernes* in Paris, felt some might dislike the building.

Like a piece of modern music, it is certain to call down anathema from a number whose ears are attuned to familiar

---

352 Howard Robertson, "Two Great Buildings of 1924", *The Architect's Journal*, Vol. 61, 7 January 1925, pp. 4-12. David Walker's essay on Sir John James Burnet in *Edwardian Architecture and Its Origins* considers the building to be "the finest expression of Burnet early modern". Alastair Service, *Edwardian Architecture and Its Origins* (Wallop, Hampshire: The Architectural Press, Ltd., 1975), pp. 192-215.

Adelaide House, London, 1925 (© RIBA Collections)

harmonies. On the other hand it will delight all those who see it the promise of something better in commercial architecture than has been even hinted in the immediate past, at least on anything like this scale… It appeals, not to sentiment, but to logic, its effects are not of picturesqueness, but of grandeur, its vitality is intense and young rather than age-old and romantic. It is a design which throws off charming courtesies and conventions and becomes boldly and frankly assertive – and why not?[353]

Robertson concluded that Burnet's work was a truly handsome structure that fulfilled its purpose by possessing all the ideals held in theory but seldom followed through in practice.

Howard Charlton Bradshaw of *The Times* thought the building's simplicity might seem stark but that in itself created a certain expression of dignity. "It is a business building and proud of it", he exclaimed.[354] The fine vertical lines, flat surfaces, numerous windows and limited ornamentation showed that the office building, as a distinctly modern problem, had been solved triumphantly by modern methods.

Vernon Blake, critic for *The Architectural Review*, disliked certain design aspects, specifically too much equal repetition and lack of fenestration variation; the principal, mausoleum-like entrance façade was too massive thereby crushing the appearance and making one feel the "sombre influence of Munich", but overall he, too, heaped praise on the structure, referring to it as a "style of architecture at one with the aesthetic of the near future".

English architects are now attacking the problem of future building formulae contemporaneously with their brethren of the Continent and the two Americas. Herein, to me,

---

353 Howard Robertson, "Two Great Buildings of 1924", *The Architect's Journal*, Vol. 61, 7 January 1925, pp. 4-12.

354 H. Charlton Bradshaw, "Buildings of the Year: Architectural Tendencies", *The Times*, 7 April 1925, p. xiii.

lies the importance, in the history of British architecture, of such essays on a considerable scale as Adelaide House.[355]

Blake did not want to belittle the building's greatness. He concluded that John Burnet and Partners had made history by giving British commercial architecture a definitively modern expression. The structure was a genuine achievement. He reminded architects that they alone controlled whether Adelaide House and similarly designed buildings would serve as the foundation for a modern tradition or be cast aside as a noble but disposable experiment.[356]

The accolades bestowed on Adelaide House still masked Britain's fragile acceptance for modernist designs. Some could argue that despite two decades of serious debate and semi-farcical predictions about what modernisms meant and its potential impact on Britain, little unfettered progress had been made. Modernisms, however, could not be defined by only one structure but by a series of buildings designed and constructed over time. It was only then that architects and society could possibly grasp the movement's significance, appreciate its meaning and determine its longevity. The war's aftermath had transfixed society to such an extent that the uncomfortableness of the present and the pining for the past could only be eased through the gradual passage of time. The war had caused a reclassification of society's boundaries – of its social norms – preventing many either to understand or to accept that quantum changes had occurred. It is unfortunate that historians who have studied Britain's quest toward architectural modernism either dismissed or ignored the morsel-like advancements society made on its path toward a new taxonomy of reality.

---

355 Vernon Blake, "Adelaide House, London", *The Architectural Review*, Vol. 57, February 1925, pp. 61-73. Blake thought that life was sad enough in many aspects so society should not insist upon sadness in art. "Can we not leave aside ponderous Germanic things and learn more of joy from the Latin peoples?"

356 Ibid. Some buildings imitated key elements of Adelaide House throughout the 1920s.

A year earlier in 1924, the British Empire Exhibition at Wembley opened to great fanfare and expectation. The entire empire, replete with its manufacturing and agricultural potential, was displayed for patrons to enjoy and to imagine the possibilities. The exhibition elevated the country's optimism about itself and the larger empire and, whether real or imagined, provided reassurance ten years after the war began that the nation and its far-flung entities were indivisibly united and richly prosperous. Except for the extensive use of concrete, particularly on some structures' exposed face work – a first for Britain – the exhibition buildings unfortunately did not offer anything architecturally inspiring. It could have been different. It should have been unique: architects showcasing modern designs juxtaposed against displays emphasizing the empire's economic capabilities. While a contemporary reviewer praised the result, even he realized the structures could have been more significant: "The result did not represent what could be done, and that while it was a milestone on the roads [sic] towards the proper treatment of concrete, it was by no means the last milestone".[357] *The Builder* made no apologies for the lack of modern design sensibilities: "A style in architecture is only created after painful and continuous efforts for years and years. Here we are in a British Exhibition, and everything from the smallest product to the biggest building must be British".[358] Once again it seemed the best excuse to turn away from modernisms was that it remained decidedly un-British. This reluctance was about to wane as Britain emerged from its imperial cocoon and participated in the architectural and design dynamics unfolding in Europe.

Reaction to the British pavilion at the 1925 *Exposition des Arts Decoratifs et Industriels Modernes* in Paris ironically accomplished what twenty years of posturing – both for and against modernisms – failed to do. It forced architects to re-evaluate long-held beliefs that modern designs amounted to nothing but the "latest

---

357 Oscar Faber, "The Concrete Buildings", *The Architectural Review*, Vol. 55, January-June, 1924, p. 221.

358 "British Empire Exhibition", *The Builder*, Vol. CXXVI, 2 May 1924, p. 721.

expression of newness and the gloss of novelty".[359] When Britain's structural apostasy was juxtaposed against the panoply of modern designs from other nations it forced a fundamental paradigm shift in the way architects perceived modernisms. Time had progressed, transgressing the past and replacing it with both the excitement and the uncertainty of the future.

Unfortunately the architects who designed the British Pavilion for the long-delayed 1925 *Exposition des Arts Decoratifs et Industriels Modernes* in Paris either were hamstrung by internal political forces and meager budgets, or lacked the courage to accept that circumstances had changed radically. The latter seems highly unlikely. The French Exposition authorities had requested all pavilion architecture clearly reflect "modern tendencies" and not derivatives or recreations from the past. In early 1924, Sir Hubert Llewellyn Smith, Chief Economic Adviser to His Majesty's Government and Chairman of the British Exposition Committee, asked the newly formed Royal Fine Arts Commission for guidance in both selecting an architect and ensuring they complied with the parameters outlined by French authorities. While the Royal Institute of British Architects chose the architects for the selection process, the Fine Arts Commission appointed the chief assessor, architect and author Harry S. Goodhart-Rendel.[360] The committee

---

359 Albert E. Richardson, "The Modern Movement in Architecture", *Journal of the Royal Institute of British Architects,* Vol. XXXI, February 1924, pp. 267-274. Read at Manchester University before the Manchester Society of Architects, 27 February 1924.

360 The five architects competing for the job included Robert Atkinson, Maxwell Ayrton, Henry Wilson & F. W. Troup, Vincent Harris and Howard Robertson & J. Murray Easton. *Records of the Royal Fine Arts Commission, Minutes,* 6 August 1924, BP 1/1, National Archives, London.

    Goodhart-Rendel served as RIBA president from 1937-1939, and in 1936 accepted the directorship of the Architectural Association School of Architecture in London. His tenure was short – he resigned two years later – due, in part, to concerns that he was stuck in the past and not 'modern' enough. Kenneth Allinson, *The Architects and Architecture of London* (Oxford: Elsevier, Ltd., 1997), pp. 234-235.

made two additional suggestions. The competitors would not be required to reproduce a specific style or historical period; all proposals would be considered as long as the design conformed to an "accepted type of British architecture". Commissioners unfortunately neither defined nor offered examples of what exactly comprised "British architecture". Moreover, it recommended architects did not copy elements or reproduce a design of a British pavilion from any previous international exhibitions. Of the five designs, Goodhart-Rendel chose the one offered by Howard Robertson and J. Murray Easton, a selection he described in a memo to the Commission as "unexpectedly easy". He added: "From whatever point of view it be regarded, one design is so very much better than the rest that I could have no possible hesitation in awarding to it the first-place in the competition".[361]

Partners since 1919, Robertson and Easton were considered by colleagues as organizing one of the most successful partnerships on record. In the firm's early years, Robertson, in particular, did much to increase awareness of architects to the architectural changes occurring in post-war Europe. A year before being selected for the British Pavilion he wrote an article for *The Architectural Review*. He argued that Britain's architectural ancestors did not imitate their ancestors the way many contemporary architects did. Instead they expressed their own minds and spirits and built in forms "that were inevitable and natural to their manner of construction, their materials and their requirements". Robertson heralded the results as "a hallmark of their particular period to their architecture". His concluding statement undoubtedly rankled all but the most forward-leaning architects. Semantics aside, Robertson had pithily summarized what architects had been debating for decades. "Our best ancestors were modernists", Robertson surmised, "so

---

361 Records of the Royal Fine Arts Commission, Minutes, 1924, BP 1/1, National Archives, London.

modernism is the best tradition".[362] His partner, J. Murray Easton, later became enamored of Scandinavian leading-edge architects Eliel Saarinen and Edvard Thomsen. A year after the Paris Exposition closed the partnership designed The Royal Horticultural Society New Halls, Westminster in London. The conservative brickwork exterior offered little clue of the interior: numerous hyperbolic arches made of reinforced concrete that proved integral to the building's unique design and aesthetic success.[363] The design won the Royal Institute of British Architects Medal in 1928 for the best building constructed that year. Both architects unfortunately failed to funnel their ample creative skills and burgeoning enthusiasm for modernist design into the British Pavilion in Paris.

After periodic delays and rescheduling due to the Great War, the much anticipated *Exposition des Arts Decoratifs et Industriels Modernes* opened in Paris on 28 April 1925.[364] Not only was post-war Paris on display, so was modernism. Buildings designed by Josef Gocar (Czechoslovakia Pavilion), Le Corbusier (Pavillon de L'Esprit Nouveau), Konstantin Melnikov (Soviet Pavilion), Jozef Czajkowski (Polish Pavilion) and Josef Hoffmann (Austrian Pavilion) made it glaringly obvious to all attendees that the new had replaced the old. The venue served as an accurate précis of modernisms' development since the Great War. The Exposition certainly impacted author Aldous Huxley who, after viewing several modernist structures and imagining the possibilities, implored the British public to loosen

---

362 Howard Robertson, "Modern Dutch Architecture", *The Architectural Review*, Vol. LIV, July-December 1923, p. 97-101

363 Howard Robertson Obituary, *The Builder*, Vol. 204, 10 May 1963, p. 915; John Murray Easton Obituary, *Journal of the Royal Institute of British Architects*, Vol. 82, September 1975, p. 6; Alan Powers, *Modern: The Modern Movement in Great Britain*, p. 15.

364 Carol S. Eliel, *L'Esprit Nouveau, Purism in Paris, 1918-1925* (Los Angeles: Los Angeles Museum of Art, 2001), p. 49. The Exposition was supposed to open in 1915 but in 1912 it was reschedule for 1916. The war obviously made this impossible so it was delayed until 1922 and then again to 1924. It finally opened in 1925.

its obsession with period and let architects think for themselves, especially regarding "good proportion, discreet adornment, pleasing material and colour".[365] "Enough good architects have already freed themselves from preoccupation with Period", Huxley wrote, "to make us look forward with high hopes to the architecture of the future".[366] Hubert de Cronin Hastings, editor of *The Architectural Review*, also was excited, pronouncing unequivocally that after visiting the Exposition a modern expression – a new rhythm – had arrived.

> If we contemplate jazz music, French furniture and painting, Swedish architecture, dress design, interior decoration, literature – whatever way we look we see new expressive forms taking over the emotional intention of old. The process is slow, but inevitable. Convalescence begins to set in after the distemper of the war, and vitality grows.[367]

While the experience of Paris acted as a catalyst for change, many in Britain still clutched firmly but a bit more hesitantly to the past.

Historians have characterized the British Pavilion as "feminine", a "deliberately frivolous and decorative effort", "strikingly un-modern", and "half-hearted in the extreme".[368] Architectural historian Mark Crinson's criticism went further: "If the British Pavilion is any indication, what 'modern' meant to British architects in 1925 was unclear and certainly was not reconcilable with what has accepted as 'national'". He concluded

---

365 Aldous Huxley, "Where Ignorance is Bliss", *The Architect's Journal*, Vol. LXII, 19 August 1925, pp. 259-260.

366 Ibid.

367 Hubert de Cronin Hastings, "Exposition Internationale Des Arts Decoratifs et Industriels Modernes: Paris, MDCCCXXV", *The Architectural Review*, Vol. LVIII, July-December 1925, p. 14.

368 *British Art and Design 1900-1960* (London: Victoria and Albert Museum, 1983), p. xii; Alan Powers, *Modern: The Modern Movement in Britain* (London: Merrell Publishers, 2005), pp. 15, 34-35.

that the structural design was as "difficult to categorize today as it was then".[369]

Contemporary British reviewers were a bit kinder. *The Builder* felt the structure reflected the spirit of the British people by expressing their sense of wanderlust and assimilation. "His [the Englishman] instinct is to go abroad", the reviewer opined, "and the hallmark of his culture lies in his gift of accepting impressions. The old-time insularity is certainly there, but it does not extend much further than to the ritualistic bath, the grey flannel trousers, and a Union Jack accent".[370] Perhaps reflecting Britain's perceived weakened position in world affairs, *The Builder* felt the building lacked "virtuosity and sophistication" and appeared "more tentative and less assured; one feels that it may make more mistakes, but it has more to say".[371] *The Architectural Review* seemed awkwardly positive about the structure, believing it was "hot from the Architectural Association pantomime".[372] It praised the architects for "the amount of detail [they] have massed in a small space" but admitted that it was "not always successful... you are at liberty to do one thing or fifty without a particular reason for any of them". Nonetheless the editor suggested that anyone who visited the pavilion "would be filled with gratitude to its designers for their pluck in carrying out with assurance a conception which a little cowardice would have killed".[373] Others probably wished the architects had acted a bit more cowardly. The French thought the magnitude of the building and the exhibits reflected the country's economic importance, but from an artistic standpoint it lacked any semblance of design revelation expected of Great Britain. One French

---

369 Mark Crinson, *Modern Architecture and the End of Empire* (Aldershot, England: Ashgate Publishing Ltd., 2003), p. 81.

370 Manning Robertson, "The British Pavilion at Paris", *The Builder*, Vol. 128, 22 May 1925, p. 788.

371 Ibid.

372 Hubert de Cronin Hastings, "A General View", *The Architectural Review*, Vol. LVIII, July-December 1925, pp. 3-19.

373 Hubert de Cronin Hastings, "The British Pavilion", *The Architectural Review*, Vol. LVIII, July-December 1925, pp. 34-36.

British Pavilion, Paris, 1925 (© RIBA Collections)

critic concluded the pavilion must have been "a fantasy... designed by a retired colonel".[374]

The British government's architectural representative, Howard C. Bradshaw, naturally praised what he termed the structure's "gay exterior" and "skillfully decorated interior", believing it made a definite contribution to the Exposition equaling the stature of other pavilions including that of France. "It was not indicative of contemporary or any other architecture in England", Bradshaw concluded, "but had tendencies which manifested themselves in the work of some of the younger school". His latter comment regarding "the younger school" may be understandable coming from an architect who had studied at the British School at Rome and became the first Rome Scholar in Architecture. Despite his affinity toward classicism, Bradshaw perceptively identified what he labeled as "a decidedly Middle European design influence" that dominated pavilion designs, especially those of Poland, Czechoslovakia, Austria and the Netherlands. Although Germany was prohibited from participating in the Exposition – as punishment for bringing about the war – Bradshaw attributed it as an important design influence that explained "much that is unexpected in the architecture of many of the adjoining countries". The "unexpected", of course, served as a euphemism for architectural modernisms.[375]

The British Pavilion was situated beautifully on the north bank of the River Seine alongside the Pont Alexandre III. The building consisted of an elongated hall with a central axis through the middle that contained the entrance hall, exhibition galleries and a general hall. The main entryway consisted of an arched doorway with a curved niche along the sides and top that contained decorative tile-like discs embedded in the structure. Painted reliefs and motifs

374 Arnold Schwartzman, *London Art Deco* (London: Aurum Press, Ltd., 2006), pp. 7-8.

375 *Reports on the Present Position and Tendencies of the Industrial Arts as Indicated at the International Exhibition of Modern Decorative and Industrial Arts, Paris, 1925* (London: Department of Overseas Trade, 1927), pp. 39-50.

ran completely along the top and bottom of the building's plain, exterior plaster construction. The three entrance hall windows were curved while the fenestration in the longer exhibition hall was rectangular, totaling three on each side. The building's roof housed a pinnacled lantern topped with a sailing ship which gave it a definite ecclesiastical touch, enabling visitors to refer to the pavilion by its nickname, "the kirk".[376]

Disappointment was not limited to the pavilion structure. *The Studio* expressed concern about the quality of the nation's decorative arts. No matter how anxious Britain was for its contributions to appear "new", it failed to break from the past. Only France, Holland, Austria, Czechoslovakia and, to a lesser extent, Belgium had "made a clean sweep of all the traditional styles" and created designs evoking the rhythmic age of modernism.[377] Most British-designed pieces consisted of Arts and Crafts style or Georgian reproductions. One exception was a desk of mahogany, camphor, and ebony gesso that was gilded with white gold. Designed by Sir Edward Maufe and made by W. Rowcliffe, it was one of the few items that compared favorably with the newest French and Continental designs.[378] *The Studio* offered cautionary advice to architects, designers, manufacturers and artisans "full of the modern spirit". Although the fashion of copying from the past was "deservedly" dead, they needed to beware of creating eccentric fantasies and novelties that were "merely freakish". Such creations would cause a disillusioned public to lose interest and turn away.[379]

376 Mark Crinson, *Modern Architecture and the End of Empire* (Aldershot, England: Ashgate Publishing Ltd., 2003), pp. 80-81; Manning Robertson, "The British Pavilion at Paris", *The Builder*, Vol. 128, 22 May 1925, p. 788.

377 Gabriel Mourey, "The Paris International Exhibition, 1925: Interior Decoration and Furnishing", *The Studio*, Vol. 90, 1925, pp. 154-157.

378 The desk resides on permanent display in the Victoria and Albert Museum, London. *British Art and Design 1900-1960* (London: Victoria and Albert Museum, 1983), p.94.

379 Gabriel Mourey, "The Paris International Exhibition, 1925: The French Buildings", *The Studio*, Vol. 90, 1925, pp. 16-21.

One patron's disappointment bordered on bewilderment. He found British efforts hardly creditable to both artists and manufacturers. The items lacked originality and design creativity and, in most instances, were badly displayed.[380] Another visitor, Sir Lawrence Weaver, architectural editor of *Country Life*, lamented that the entire purpose of the Exposition was lost on the people it was supposed to stimulate: the home goods manufacturer. He appreciated that critics and competent artists alike regarded the revolt against tradition either as a mere passing fancy that probably should be ignored, or as a truly revolutionary movement to be fought and defeated. Unfortunately for Weaver, the majority had dismissed the international effort as negligible simply because it was modern. If manufacturers ignored the quantum changes – "the pulse of modernity" – throbbing within the design, art and architectural disciplines they did so at their own peril. Moreover, implored Weaver, if they visited the Exposition they would be shocked at the accomplishments of their European counterparts. Britain might continue churning out Chippendale chairs, willow-pattern plates and Jacobean umbrella stands, he argued, but there was no guarantee the public would continue purchasing reproductions or antique derivatives. As far as Europe was concerned, the market for such items was dead already.[381]

A month after Weaver's comment was published in *The Times*, *The Architect* responded with a scathing review of the book *The Modern Style* by Ernest Benn. The book focused on a number of modern designs by French architects and furniture designers. The reviewer thought the book helpful by serving as both a warning and a reminder that "even in art matters there is a movement towards the goal of Nihilism". A proper Englishman, the reviewer surmised, would not be drawn to such crude and bizarre fancies.

---

380 Sydney H. Paviere, "Letters to the Editor: Art in Industry", *The Times*, 5 October 1925, p. 10.

381 Lawrence Weaver, "Letters to the Editor: Modern Art in Industry. Lessons of Paris Exhibition", *The Times*, 3 October 1925, p. 6.

The piano designed by Rene Prou was a "coarse monstrosity", a table of Robert Delaunay's resembled "an alter in the Stone Age", and few could find comfort in the armchairs of Pierre Legrain or feel at home in the villa designed by Andre Lurcat. The reviewer confessed that he did not understand how Lawrence Weaver could defend such eccentric designs. All would fail miserably if offered for sale to the British public. "We do not think there is any practical gain in eliminating all moulded or carved forms or ornament", the reviewer concluded. "Surfaces still remain to be dusted and cleaned, and there is certainly nothing to please the eye or to delight the fancy".[382]

After reviewing the vast assemblage of French interior designs, Vernon Blake of *The Architectural Review* asked somewhat rhetorically, but in a less harsher tone than the article discussed above in *The Architect*, whether an Englishman who visited the modern French *ensembliers* could live among such opulent surroundings void of coziness. "Our Englishman", he reminded readers, "mindful of fireside joys, of capacious easy chairs, will, perhaps, admire, then turn aside and leave such artificialities to the exhibition and to France".[383] Despite his hearth and home nationalism, Blake felt Britain could learn much from the sleekness and bold simplicity of the French but only if it concentrated on the genuine innovators striving toward perfection and ignored the second-rate imitators. Such action would enhance British architecture and design and help reclaim its rightful position as an originator of what became the modern movement.

Others who visited the Exposition felt Britain's domestic goods manufacturers remained ignorantly unaware of the extent to which modern design and functionalism had replaced past designs. Such unfamiliarity enabled rivals on the Continent to

---

382 "Book Reviews: *The Modern Style*", *The Architect*, Vol. CXIV, 6 November 1925, pp. 332-333.

383 Vernon Blake, "Modern Decorative Art-II", *The Architectural Review*, Vol. LVIII, July-December 1925, pp. 181-186.

reap the benefits of being on the cusp of change. The attractiveness of the new had become far more encompassing than many British business leaders had realized. London executive Frank Warner attended the Exposition and came away quite impressed, determined to embrace the radical changes under way.

> The efforts of designers have been directed towards securing the charm associated with harmonious schemes for the internal decoration of rooms, including doors, windows, furniture, carpets and hangings, glass, pottery, metal work, and other details. In some cases striking and pleasing results have been obtained on new and original lines to the entire exclusion of anything reminiscent of past periods. This is a considerable achievement and I have been sufficiently impressed with what has been done to send my leading designers to Paris so that they may grasp the trend of the development which is taking place and be prepared to play their part in it.[384]

He encouraged other businessmen to attend the event so they could judge the magnitude of developments that he believed had a far-reaching character and elastic longevity.[385]

William Moorcroft, founder of Moorcroft Pottery in Stoke-on-Trent, thought differently. He believed it unfortunate if Britain felt forced to embrace the "pulse of modernity". Moorcroft implored his countrymen to be true to themselves, perhaps paraphrasing poet Rupert Brooke's immortal lines, "by remembering ever that England is England". To do anything less would be injurious to the country's success. Britain's reliance on tradition worked to its advantage, he argued, especially since France and other European

---

384 Frank Warner, "Letter to the Editor: Modern Art in Industry", *The Times*, 14 October 1925, p. 17.
385 Ibid.

nations had embraced modern designs so completely. Moorcroft encouraged craftsmen and designers to visit the Exposition so they would know what to avoid.[386]

Cecil Harcourt Smith, the recently retired director of the Victoria and Albert Museum and Vice-Chairman of the British Institute of Industrial Art, had served as a consultant to the Department of Overseas Trade during the Paris Exposition. In a "Letter to the Editor" of *The Times*, Smith conceded that Britain's efforts may not have showcased modernism as well as other nations, but certainly were "worthy of comparison". He believed that for twenty years, but certainly since the war, a new attitude had emerged within the design community: continually question tradition and other time-honoured principles from the past. These radical precepts, he felt, proved especially difficult for Britain to follow especially since the war.

> The fact is, the pulse of modernity is just now beating somewhat feverishly: such conditions are conducive to the seeing of visions and the dreaming of dreams: and the visions and dreams are not always such as one would wish to come true.

The country's contentedness with the past, Smith argued, prevented it from experimenting because so many individuals could not find either promise or fulfillment in the present or the future. It was as if a deep, societal depression had descended upon the country. Although modernity had infiltrated almost every aspect of design, Smith felt no one could state unhesitatingly that the movement would endure. "[W]e are as yet too close to the new movement for prophecy, or even for selection", Smith wrote. "We need time to give it a due perspective and to allow it… to settle down".[387]

---

386 William Moorcroft, "Letter to the Editor: Modern Art in Industry", *The Times*, 7 October 1925, p. 10.

387 Cecil Harcourt Smith, "Letters to the Editor: Industrial Art. Modernity and Tradition. Lessons of the Paris Exhibition", *The Times*, 3 November 1925, p. 10.

And so for one of Britain's important trade officials and cultural arbiters, only time would divulge whether modernisms would endure beyond the perceived excitement of Paris. The wait for Britain, however, was shorter than Smith and perhaps many others had imagined. The wide-embracing tentacles of modernisms had grabbed hold and would not loosen their grip.

The most prescient analysis appeared in the final report published in 1927 by Sir Hubert Llewellyn Smith, Chief Economic Advisor to His Majesty's Government and Chairman of the recently founded British Institute of Industrial Art. While the report offered a comprehensive economic and business viability review of the Exposition, it was the thirty-eight page *Introductory Summary* where he grappled with the troublesome issues surrounding Britain's laden movement in accepting design modernisms. Smith appreciated that the Exposition's purpose was to highlight products that fulfilled a practical need while simultaneously demonstrating originality with a "modern tendency". He understood the juxtaposition of traditional versus contemporary designs and how it influenced decisions of both the manufacturer and the consumer. Smith's chief concern was whether the design revelations of Paris were a temporary infatuation or a significant change in course and direction for industrial art and architecture. It was the essence of his thesis and something he emphasized from the beginning.

> If we could view in imagination a cross-section of the stream of art production in any normal period we should find a central mass or nucleus representing a slowly changing and developing tradition, while dispersed around it would be a number of more or less erratic deviations from standard, representing the conscious or unconscious attempts to break free from customary practice... [T]hese experimental departures from the normal are of very great interest, if their significance is rightly understood, and if they are viewed in their proper relation to the main stream of development.

But the Paris rule undoubtedly involved the danger that, by excluding or discouraging much normal modern work, it might contribute undue weight to the divergences, and thus give a misleading impression of the strength and direction of modern art tendencies.

An important concern of Smith's was the economic viability of the "exhibition pieces" once they were exposed to, what he termed, "the blast of economic forces". Did these products represent new and permanent changes in the art and design history of the world or were they merely beautiful and inspirational objects that would be unsustainable and useless in everyday life? While he admitted he could not predict the future or issue a firm verdict one way or another, Smith acknowledged that several of the authors who contributed to the report believed the Exposition marked not merely "a transient movement, but a real renaissance, destined to exercise a permanent influence on the course of art development and to give rise to a new style". Other contributors interpreted the event differently, considering it as nothing more than an "intermediate stage of progress towards a yet unrealized synthesis". These two differing points of view, one pointing toward definite achievement and the other offering inspirational hope for some future date, ironically were the same conclusions reached by the architectural profession after twenty years of vigorous debate. Britain's battle to go modern finally had come to a head.

Smith was troubled by those who were impressed by the excellent craftsmanship of the items displayed in the British Pavilion, for he was struck by the dullness, the aloofness and the absence of any spirit of adventure in either the objects or the design. He wondered whether greater lessons needed to be learned from these inherent "defects" in the exhibition pieces. Smith appreciated that the most obvious reason for the lack of design initiative was the "strong continuity of traditional life". The "soundness of British art" and the comparatively small degree to which the culture had been impacted by what he called "the explosive forces originating or culminating in the war" had enabled the culture to continue unabated. While Smith considered tradition an attribute, he felt it reflected a condition of tiredness, of weakness, and waning vitality, particularly regarding the lack of collaboration between artists and manufacturers. A potential cause for the country's poor showing revolved around its indifference toward the European art and design movements that occurred earlier in the century. Smith believed Britain's unreceptiveness to movements from abroad had enabled it to be comparatively immune from any direct impact either before or after the war. Interestingly, while he had not paid close attention to modernisms' development earlier in the century – his positions in the Board of Trade and as the head of the British Economic Section at the Versailles Peace Conference may have kept him isolated from the main currents of cultural thought – he found little difficulty trumpeting the Arts and Crafts Movement's influence on Europe. After viewing product and building designs in several pavilions, Smith saw "abundant signs" and "clear evidence" of Britain's earlier successes. Flummoxed as to whether Britain's less-than-impressive showing characterized a mark of high or of low vitality, he asked a series of rhetorical but pertinent questions.

> How far do they [the poor-quality products] reflect the qualities of sanity, restraint and continuity of tradition which are signs of health and power? And how far may the relative imperviousness of British Industrial Art to the forces which have been sweeping over the Continent of Europe, be rightly ascribed to the superior resisting power of a sound and healthy organism to the microbes of disease?

> How far on the other hand do the qualities observed in the British section imply a degree of rigidity and ossification

and an enfeeblement of the power of reacting to external stimulus which are well-known marks of impaired health and organic decay?

How far again is the British reluctance to break with past practice a sign of the vigorous persistence of living tradition, or how far is it the mere clinging of a parasitic plant which has lost the power of independent growth and life?[388]

Smith confessed he could not begin to anticipate the responses. The only certainty was that if the examination was thorough and impartial the answers would vary widely. When the report was published in 1927, Smith's intellectual curiosity obviously had been awakened by his Paris experience. He thought that merely participating in the cultural self-examination process would be as fruitful as finding exacting answers. Smith understood the war had caused, as he termed it, "a complete break in the normal evolution of political and social thought and aspirations". While he may have thought Britain had been spared – it certainly had in regards to physical devastation – most, if not all, of Europe had been destroyed physically, ripped apart socially, and impaired mentally. The war had acted as a fiery catalyst for cultural modernisms, quickly replacing the vacuum and filling the void caused by four years of warfare. Britain's cultural establishment finally realized that the fertile grounds of modernisms sown earlier in the century in Europe and something it had resisted so fervently for so long had become ubiquitous by the mid-1920s. Its pervasiveness and longevity could no longer be denied.

Shortly before the Exposition opened, "A Letter to the Editor" in *The Times* broadly attacked recently built structures in London including some particularly unflattering comments about the

---

388 *Reports on the Present Position and Tendencies of the Industrial Arts as Indicated at the International Exhibition of Modern Decorative and Industrial Arts, Paris, 1925* (London: Department of Overseas Trade, 1927), pp. 9-38.

Cenotaph and Adelaide House. Essayist and poet, Loren H. B. Knox, wrote that their style was

> a thoroughly ugly, coarse soulless style having run its course in Germany and America, conforming to represent tasteless ideas of indigenous simplicity, sincerity and particularly, but proving the incapacity of the present even to sense beauty of line, proportion or ornament. In this type, masses are crude, blotchy, heavy, with cutting angles, giving a sense of harshness which must disgust posterity, if it has any sound judgement... As this age has no soul to produce an original architecture, better 'adapt' old lovely styles to present needs than mistakenly to strain after a 'new', which, affecting Egyptian pylon motives, is neither new, indigenous, spiritual or graceful. There is no virtue in ugliness because it is utilitarian... There will be no essence, soul or attractiveness left in London unless architects quit this craze, and learn that they cannot mentally force a mode in architecture.[389]

Editors of *The Builder* fervently disagreed, and wrote a rebuttal that reflected how far the acceptance of modern architecture devoid of "old lovely styles" had come since the end of the war: "Work ahead of its time is always abused, but it does not follow that it is ahead of its time merely because it is abused... [W]e believe that the vast majority of architects will accept the abuse as a sign that architecture is at last evolving into something of value".[390]

Although modernisms lacked unequivocal acceptance, its time

---

389 Loren H. B. Knox, "Letters to the Editor: Modern Architecture", *The Times*, 27 May 1925, p. 14.

390 "Ugly Modern Architecture", *The Builder*, Vol. XXVIII, 5 June 1925, p. 856. The specific article appeared in *The Times* on 27 May 1925 in the "Letters to the Editor" section, p. 14. Written by Loren H. B. Knox of Queen's Gate, London, it was entitled "Modern Architecture".

in Britain finally had arrived. The difficulty that modernist-leaning architects faced was they had no ancestry, no past. Instead of being a liability it soon became an asset as planning for a different future began to replace the nation's obsession-like propensity to replicate and to prop up the past at any cost.

6

Epilogue

"For the modern structure a modern beat is required, not necessarily jazz nor even purer forms of syncopation, but quite as different in accent as these are from the solemn harmonies of the classics with their recognized beats in a composition".[391]

— The Architectural Review, 1929

"Whether it is possible to 'go modern' and still 'be British' is a question vexing quite a few people today… The battle lines have been drawn up: internationalism versus an indigenous culture; renovation versus conservatism; the industrial versus the pastoral; the functional versus the futile".[392]

— Paul Nash, Artist, 1932

---

391 Myras, "The New Rhythm", *The Architectural Review*, Vol. LXV, January-June 1929, pp. 194-195.

392 Paul Nash, "'Going Modern' and 'Being British'", *Week-end Review*, 12 March 1932, p. 322.

The levels of interest shown by architects in modernisms gradually increased after the Exposition. Paris legitimized modernisms' existence – a nodal point in its forward movement. Although not totally eradicated, any impulse toward revivalism after 1925 proved anemic. After decades of intense discussion, woeful indecision, world war and societal reconstruction, many began to appreciate that despite its awkward unpleasantness modernisms accurately reflected the harmony and perhaps disharmony of the present age. It was not necessarily inimical to British traditions and, given a chance, could fit nicely into contemporary customs, habits and lifestyles. If presented properly modernisms could satisfy society's new found needs. Standing still and pining for the past was no longer an option. While it lacked unconditional acceptance modernisms had obtained a certain level of credence empowering some architects to assume the responsibility for propelling the movement forward, to design and to build for the present. There also was increased belief that modern designs could succeed despite protestations from traditionalists who *never* had welcomed experimentation. Progressives understood that modern architecture eventually would emerge and be recognized as part of the transcendent building designs reflected throughout history. A minority even anticipated the possibility, no matter how unpalatable, that eponymous local and national architecture could disappear under modern conditions, making domestic and commercial structures similar throughout the world.[393] While a new creative era certainly had surfaced, its impact was not blatantly obvious. Any forward movement resembled more of a disciplined march than a triumphant demonstration. "Though to many it may seem lacking the spirit of adventure", reflected the editors of *The Builder*, "[it] at least affords a path of safety – free from deadly

---

393 Frederick Etchells, "Exhibitions at the Royal Academy & the Royal Institute of British Architects", *The Architectural Review*, Vol. LXV, January-June 1929, pp. 278-282; F. R. Yerbury, *Modern European Buildings* (London: Victor Gollancz, 1928), pp. 5-6.

antiquarianism on the one hand, and from fantastic originality on the other. Today we are going through a period of transition, and many of the architectural conceptions of the confessed modernist must be of an experimental nature".[394] Supporters of modernisms felt confident that after so many chaotic efforts to achieve something new, a sound, sane and satisfactory result would emerge. It revolved around architects and society accepting a new taxonomy to begin a reluctant but necessary transition toward a modern reality. "If we can make up our minds to turn our heads from the past to the future", Professor Beresford Pite told colleagues at the Royal Institute of British Architects, "to think of art as men of science think of science, of our work as being progressive instead of retrogressive, there may be some hope".[395] Ironically, by the time Britain began to feel somewhat "comfortable" with modernisms, European architects had advanced the design process even further. Architectural historian John W. Summerson wrote in 1930 that soon after the *Exposition des Arts Decoratifs et Industriels Modernes* "several architects threw off the remaining shackles of stylistic handling and became geometricians pure and simple".[396] If British architects had learned anything since 1925, they came to understand the dynamic fluidity of modernisms' early years and no longer wanted to be left behind. They needed to participate.

Despite his whimsical design of the British Pavilion in Paris, Howard Robertson accurately understood the ramifications of the "before and after" demarcation – the new taxonomy of reality – created by the Great War. In March 1927, Robertson proffered his ideas in an address before colleagues at the Royal Institute of British Architects.

---

394 "Modernism", *The Builder*, Vol. CXXXIV, 17 October 1930, p. 639.

395 Beresford Pite, "Modernism in Architecture", *Journal of the Royal Institute of British Architects*, Vol. XXXV, 9 June 1928, pp. 511-523.

396 John W. Summerson, "A Cubist Architect", *The Builder*, Vol. CXXXIX, 19 December 1930, p. 1038.

The war, with all its evil, has clarified certain issues. It has led to independent thought, to a distrust of perpetual compromise, to a questioning of everything, including the authority of architectural traditions. Before the war experiment was going on, originators were at work. But since the war, greater recognition has been accorded to the pioneers, and more designers have joined their ranks.

Robertson praised the work of what he called "modernist extremists" because their work had acted as a spur to others. Although he did not identify them individually, Robertson confessed that Britain had "one or two such spurs" and while they may never be popular, "they keep the others pushing forward along the road of progress".[397] Such an admission would not have been uttered at a Royal Institute of British Architects' meeting five, ten or fifteen years earlier.

Both Howard Robertson and *The Builder* were correct. During the post-Paris Exposition phase and into the early 1930s there was an edge-way penetration of modernisms in British building design. French architect and provocateur Le Corbusier's (Charles-Edouard Jeanneret-Gris) seminal work, *Vers une Architecture* (*Toward an Architecture*, sometimes translated as *Towards a New Architecture*) originally was published in France in 1923. Reaction to his design Pavillon de l'Esprit Nouveau at the Paris Exposition generated much discussion within the British contingent. What was more important than whether British architects believed in or liked the design was that architect and former Vorticist artist, Frederick Etchells, set out almost immediately upon returning from Paris and translated Le Corbusier's book. Etchells's diligent efforts were subsequently published in 1927. He followed up this

---

397 Howard Robertson, "Modern French Architecture", *Journal of the Royal Institute of British Architects*, Vol. XXXIV, 19 March 1927, pp. 323-337. Unfortunately a clash of personalities between Robertson and Coates kept Robertson out of the MARS Group when it was founded in 1933.

achievement in 1929 by translating and writing an introduction to Le Corbusier's earlier work, *L'Urbanisme* (1924), published in English as *The City of Tomorrow and Its Planning*. These events demonstrated that while Le Corbusier's designs and the philosophy behind them may not have been attempted in Britain immediately, architects finally realized that modernisms were alive, dynamic and adaptable to modern ways of living; a new beginning that needed fresh understanding. Even detractors found difficulty denying that Le Corbusier's musings were causing seminal changes to architectural thought. It appeared that Britain's insularity and refined smugness was diminishing rapidly. These publications were significant because no such clamoring existed in 1908 or 1913 to translate or to publish Adolf Loos's influential modernism treatise, *Ornament und Verbrechen* (*Ornament and Crime*). Neither Loos nor his work were mentioned in any proceedings of the Royal Institute of British Architects prior to 1914, and no architect or publishing house thought it important enough to make the book available in English.

The era's energized creativeness enabled the construction of several noteworthy buildings as architects slowly relinquished the stranglehold the past had held for so long on the profession. The hurdle of modernisms' acceptance had been scaled. British architects finally emerged from the professional wilderness after decades of wallowing in indecisiveness. In late 1931 Raymond Unwin, known internationally as a respected advocate and expert on town planning, addressed colleagues at the Royal Institute of British Architects. His presidential address signified how far the profession had advanced since those heady and confident days before 1914.

As architects, too, we must be thrilled by the daring character of many of the new buildings springing up around us; and fascinated by the heated discussion which they aroused. Terms like functionalism and traditionalism were flung about by the several protagonists with a vigour that proved architecture to be, if not a living art, at least a lively one![398]

Such an admission helped move progressive architects from an adversarial position on the prickly margins to a respective position near the vital center.

Most, if not all, of the structures highlighted below would have been unthinkable, if not impossible, a few years earlier. Most have withstood the test of time. Many "monuments to modernisms" feature regularly in surveys of Britain's early modernist designs and architecture, and because nothing new can be added, lengthy discussion and detailed analysis of their deserved significance will be reduced.

Surprisingly it was the Crittall Manufacturing Company (a metal window and door frame manufacturer) in 1919 that spawned an early entry into modernist architecture when it designed and constructed several semi-detached and terraced workers' cottages in Braintree, Essex. The structures consisted of plain concrete blocks, diagonal metal windows and metal door frames, exposed lintels and a light handrail that ran around a flat roof. The interior floors were poured concrete. One architectural historian has noted that the design was "prophetic of forms which have been assumed to be of Continental origins".[399]

W. J. Bassett-Lowke's house, "New Ways", Northampton (1925-1926), designed by German native Peter Behrens, was considered the first modernist home in Britain. *The Architectural Review* believed it symbolized "a new phase of thought".

A hasty estimate will either condemn 'New Ways' as an

---

398 "Dr. Raymond Unwin's Presidential Address at the RIBA", *The Architect's Journal*, Vol. 74, 4 November 1931, pp. 620-621; Raymond Unwin Obituary, *Journal of the Royal Institute of British Architects*, Vol. 47, 15 July 1940, p. 210.

399 Jeremy Gould, *Modern Houses in Britain, 1919-1939* (London: Society of Architectural Historians of Great Britain, 1977), pp. 10-12.

excrescence on the landscape, or the older houses as out of date and lacking in comfort and utility, and therefore beauty. But a more mature judgment will realize that the somewhat bizarre exterior of the new is conditioned not so much by the demands of internal efficiency as by the fact that its owner desired an exercise in modernity.[400]

As Alan Powers has argued, "New Ways" had a strong and enduring influence on British domestic architecture.[401] Its completion ushered in a wave of design commissions for upper-middle class individuals who wanted cutting-edge, modernist homes. Whether they appreciated the significance of modernisms or simply wanted to impress "cultural elites" remains debatable.

In 1926, W. F. Crittall entered the fray again when he approached Thomas S. Tait of John Burnet & Partners to design several homes for workers and managers near the company's new facility at Silver End Garden Village, Essex. Crittall gave Tait a liberal remit allowing *Country Life* to comment:

[A]t the outset it must be stated that he [Tait] has done so not with the ideas of producing anything that is freakish, but frankly as a logical and practical expression of design and building in the spirit of our own day. He has approached his problem in just the same way as a motor car designer but supplemented by those aesthetic principles which form part of an architect's make-up.[402]

One of the first homes completed at Silver End was asymmetrically designed, comprising of white rendered brickwork, a flat roof and,

---

400 Shilhouette, "New Ways: The House of W. J. Bassett-Lowke, Esq., Northampton", *The Architectural Review*, Vol. LX, July-December 1926, pp. 175-179.

401 Alan Powers, *Modern: The Modern Movement in Great Britain*, p. 15.

402 Randal Phillips, "Some Houses at Silver End Garden Village, Essex", *Country Life*, Vol. LXIV, 27 October 1928, pp. 601-602.

the soon-to-be iconic component of modern homes, the horizontal casement windows without the traditional vertical glazing bars. Other homes in the village were more symmetrical and contained "V" shaped windows and entrance canopies obviously "borrowed" from Behrens's "New Ways". The homes at Silver End and "New Ways" were the first modern buildings that utilized extensive publicity and in so doing became, as an historian has noted, "the ideal of modern architecture to the public and to much of the profession".[403]

"High and Over", Buckinghamshire (1928-1930), designed by Amyas Connell, Basil Ward and Colin Lucas, contained a French Cubist garden; however, it was the flat roof, glass staircase and horizontal windows that caused a stir and raised concerns about future modernist projects.[404] The Daily Express Building (1929-1932), completed by the firm Ellis and Clarke with Evan Owen Williams serving as a consulting engineer, had exterior walls clad totally of glass – a first for Britain.[405] Elizabeth Scott's bold and impressive geometric design of the Royal Shakespeare Theatre at Stratford-upon-Avon (1929-1932), was well ahead of its time or, as Alan Powers conceded, "was as 'advanced' as could have been found at the time of the competition in 1929... "[406] Architect/artist Frederick Etchells remarked that despite being an experiment in uniqueness the details of the upper facade resembled the less admirable side of Teutonic design.[407] The BBC's weekly publication, *The Listener*, praised the structure believing it succeeded at being

---

403 Jeremy Gould, *Modern Houses in Britain, 1919-1939*, pp. 10-12.

404 Boris Ford, editor, *The Cambridge Guide to the Arts in Britain, Vol. 8, The Edwardian Age and the Inter War Years* (Cambridge: Cambridge University Press, 1989), p. 238; Alan Powers, *Modern: The Modern Movement in Great Britain*, pp. 88-89.

405 Alan Powers, *Modern: The Modern Movement in Great Britain*, pp. 24, 220-221.

406 Ibid, p. 14.

407 Frederick Etchells, "Exhibitions at the Royal Academy & the Royal Institute of British Architects", *The Architectural Review*, Vol. LXV, January-June 1929, pp. 278-282.

a theatre built of brick "without making the slightest pretense at being anything else… " The reviewer's conclusion encapsulated the essence of Britain's battle to go modern when he commented that Scott's design was "perhaps the most honest building of our generation, and in its freedom from either modernist quirks or verbose emphasis it is also characteristically English".[408] The difficult slog was nearly over: it was modernist without being weird, traditional without being too adorned with ornamentation and, most importantly for some, uniquely nationalistic. Harry S. Goodhart-Rendel's St. Olaf House, Hay's Wharf, London (1930-1931), with its overall Art Deco design and elements of Medieval Gothic contrasted nicely with the much-celebrated Adelaide House directly across the River Thames.[409] Raymond McGrath favorably described Amyas Connell's design, "The White House", Haslemere, Surrey (1931-1932), as "more like an invention by Picasso than a home".[410] Marshall Sisson's design for the home of Arnold Walter Lawrence, Thomas Edward Lawrence's (Lawrence of Arabia) younger brother on Madingley Road, Cambridge (1931-1932), invoked a De Stijl style consisting of contrasting brick, complete with windows enfolding the building's corners.[411] "Lawn Road Flats", Hampstead, London (1933-1934), by Wells Coates epitomized functional modernism. With its built-in furniture and minimalist interior design, it served as "an essay in the economy of space".[412] Walter Gropius, Marcel Breuer and Laszlo Moholy-Nagy purchased units in this iconic and either much-loved or much-loathed building. Russian-born Berthold Lubetkin designed the first of two apartment blocks, "Highpoint

---

408 Christopher Hussey, "The New Shakespeare Memorial Theatre", *The Listener*, Vol. II, No. 171, 20 April 1932, pp. 555-557.

409 Alan Powers, *Modern: The Modern Movement in Britain*, p. 124.

410 Ibid, p. 90.

411 Ibid, pp. 214-215.

412 "Obituaries, Wells Wintemute Coates", *Journal of the Royal Institute of British Architects*, Vol. LXV, 1958, p. 357.

1", Highgate, London (1933-1935). Highly praised at the time by Le Corbusier, some architectural historians consider it "the single most celebrated modernist building of the 1930s".[413] And finally, Erich Mendelsohn's and Serge Chermayeff's De La Warr Pavilion Marina, Bexhill, East Sussex (1934-1935), replete with mural by modernist painter Edward Wadsworth and bespoke furniture by Alvar Aalto, served as one of the truly iconic modernist structures of the thirties.[414]

Additional inroads were made with the founding of special interest organizations comprised exclusively of professional architects and artists including sculptors and painters. The longevity and influence of each organization varied widely but all contributed something, whether individually or collectively, to increasing the cultural legitimacy and general acceptance of modern architecture and modern art. Almost immediately after the war in 1919, Wyndham Lewis attempted to resurrect the Vorticist movement with Group X but after one exhibition and just two issues of the journal, *The Tyro*, it collapsed. Another group, the Seven and Five Society, also founded in 1919 survived until 1935, and consisted originally of seven painters and five sculptors, mainly ex-servicemen who lacked any desire to re-enter the conventional workforce. It struggled for influence initially but its importance increased as the decade progressed. Its membership eventually became more diverse and its leadership more dynamic.[415] None of these early post-war groups had architects on its membership rolls. This oversight was corrected later with the founding of two organizations that chose to be a bit more inclusive.

Founded in 1933, The Modern Architectural Research Group, known as MARS, represented British interest at the

---

413 Alan Powers, *Modern: The Modern Movement in Britain*, p. 170.

414 Richard Weston, *Modernism* (London: Phaidon Press, Ltd., 1996), pp. 174-178. Earl de la Warr, the mayor of Bexhill, commissioned the seafront pavilion.

415 Charles Harrison, *English Art and Modernism, 1900-1939* (Bloomington, Indiana: Indiana University Press, 1981), pp. 164-165.

Congres Internationaux de l'Architecture Moderne headquartered in Switzerland. The group's purpose was to study the variety of issues affecting modern architecture and find solutions or recommend alternatives. Poor funding, time restraints and personal egos limited its ability to make great strides but it achieved a modicum of success by sustaining the faith of modern architects, fostering meaningful discussions, raising public awareness and creating a certain level of professional camaraderie. In an early attempt to take MARS mainstream, Frances R. S. Yorke proudly announced in the BBC's publication, *The Listener*, that "a new British architectural Group had been formed by Wells Coates".[416] He promised more information would be forthcoming in future issues. The organization remained active until 1957.[417] "This was the most substantial gathering of the modernists against whom conventional society's doors seemed barred", wrote historian David Dean, "or at least by whom society was determined not to have its doors designed".[418] While Wells Coates served as its first chairman, some of the other sixty members included Edwin Maxwell Fry, Frances R. S. Yorke, Godfrey Samuel, Sir Owen Williams, Colin Lucas, Amyas Connell, Basil Ward, and Godfrey Samuel. John Betjeman and Hubert de Cronin Hastings, both of *The Architectural Review*, soon became active members. As the 1930s progressed, leading modern architects Serge Chermayeff and Berthold Lubetkin, émigrés from Germany and Russia respectively, joined the organization after arriving in Britain.[419] These architects

---

416 F. R. S Yorke, "Points From Letters", *The Listener*, Vol. IX, No. 225, 3 May 1933, p. 718.

417 For detailed analysis of the founding and accomplishments of MARS see Elizabeth Darling's article, "Institutionalizing English Modernism 1924-33: From the Vers Group to MARS" in *Architectural History*, Vol. 55, 2012, pp. 299-320.

418 David Dean, *The Thirties: Recalling the English Architectural Scene* (London: Trefoil Books, 1983), p. 112.

419 Boris Ford, editor, *The Cambridge Guide to the Arts in Britain, Vol. 8, The Edwardian Age and the Inter War Years* (Cambridge: Cambridge University Press, 1989), pp. 212-245; David Dean, *The Thirties: Recalling the English Architectural Scene* (London: Trefoil Books, 1983), pp. 112-113.

not only had been immersed in European modernisms but had several design accomplishments to their credit. Soon both men made profound and indelible contributions to British architecture.

Also in 1933, artist Paul Nash announced in a letter to *The Times* the formation of another new artistic group, Unit One.

> Unit One may be said to stand for the expression of a truly contemporary spirit for that thing which is recognized as peculiarly of *today* in painting, sculpture and architecture... The formation of Unit One is a method of concentrating certain individual forces, a hard defense, a compact wall against the tide, behind which development can proceed and experiment continue.[420]

Membership reflected the diversity of the group's three main disciplines. The sculptors included Henry Moore and Barbara Hepworth; the painters consisted of Edward Wadsworth, Ben Nicholson, Paul Nash, Tristram Hillier, Edward Burra, John Bigge and John Armstrong, while Wells Coates and Colin Lucas rounded out the membership as the architects. The Mayor Gallery on Cork Street in Mayfair, London, served as the group's headquarters and where members regularly displayed their work.[421]

Some of Unit One's major accomplishments before it dissolved in 1935 was a London Exhibition at the Mayor Gallery, a road tour and corresponding exhibition in Liverpool, Manchester, Hanley, Derby, Swansea and Belfast, and a well received book edited by Herbert Read highlighting each member's artistic and design philosophy including photographs of seminal works.[422]

---

420 Letters to the Editor: "Unit One A New Group of Artists", *The Times*, 12 June 1933, p. 10.

421 Herbert Read, editor, *Unit 1: The Modern Movement in English Architecture, Painting and Sculpture* (London: Cassell and Company, Ltd., 1934), pp. 1-13.

422 Ibid. Mark Glazebrook, *Unit One: Spirit of the 30's* (London: The Mayor Gallery, May-June 1984).

Decades later, architect Colin Lucas recalled that the purpose of the countrywide tour "was to familiarise the British public with modern art... [I]t was a sort of advertising campaign, and it did have a very big effect in introducing modern art; after all there were some pretty good people".[423] In characteristic form, Lucas was being modest about his contributions to British modernisms. In 1930, he designed and built the first modern concrete house in England, "Noah's House" in Bourne End. He followed this in 1933 with "The Hopfield" in St. Mary's Platt, Wrotham, Kent. Both were cutting-edge modern designs. He later joined the pioneering firm which became Connell, Ward and Lucas which was responsible for "High and Over", among others.

Although some critics and historians have undervalued Unit One's contribution to the modernist struggle, the group made its fervent plea for understanding heard by many diverse groups throughout Britain. And despite society's preoccupation with pressing domestic issues and foreign affairs and the organization's short existence, one historian has argued rather convincingly that Unit One succeeded by confronting and attacking its common enemy directly – those forces of indifference, antagonism and ridicule that despised the modern movement.[424] The group's most important legacy, however, may have been demonstrating that modernisms encouraged disparate and contradictory approaches, directions, sentiments and philosophies. No mandate existed as there had been in the past for the "correct" way to design a building, to carve or to mold a sculpture or to paint a canvas. Although this philosophy had been present since the movement's inception, entrenched reactionary forces had made little effort to comprehend that modernisms were not monolithic. The exigencies of the Great War and the new world created in its aftermath

---

423 "A Modern Briton", *Architect's Journal*, Vol. 179, 9 May 1984, pp. 28-29.
424 Mark Glazebrook, *Unit One: Spirit of the 30's* (London: The Mayor Gallery, May-June 1984), p. 9.

only exacerbated the problem. Unit One's strength was strategic, Herbert Read argued in 1934: "To form a point in the forward thrust of modernism in architecture, painting and sculpture, and to harden this point in the fires of criticism and controversy. Such an aim is not only perfectly legitimate, it is commendable".[425]

While these aforementioned organizations helped advance the acceptance of modernisms, their exclusivity – except perhaps for Unit One – unfortunately prevented the development of a more broadly-based understanding. This issue was rectified somewhat in 1922 with the founding of the British Broadcasting Corporation (BBC) and the new medium of the wireless radio. In 1922, a total of 35,744 wireless licenses were granted throughout the country. The number of owners increased steadily in the coming years so that by 1926 over 2 million licenses had been approved.[426] These statistical totals included only the number of wireless sets and not the number of people listening which obviously would have been greater. By 1930, the BBC had become an important leader and genuine supporter for the cause of modernisms throughout Britain, interpreting it as more than a transitory style. Its radio programs often contained subject matter concerning architecture and design including lectures and debate transcripts that pitted traditionalists against modernists. Moreover, the corporation's weekly subscription periodical, *The Listener*, first published in January 1929, regularly included articles on the most current and controversial issues surrounding modernisms. As one of three publications of the BBC (*Radio Times* was founded in 1923 and *World Radio* was founded in 1925), *The Listener* became a widely respected publication. While its content appealed to what one historian labeled as "the intelligent listener", it nonetheless had a strong following that experienced

---

425 Herbert Read, editor, *Unit 1: The Modern Movement in English Architecture, Painting and Sculpture* (London: Cassell and Company, Ltd., 1934), p. 12.
426 Asa Briggs, *The Birth of Broadcasting, Vol. 1* (Oxford: Oxford University Press, 1995), p. 17.

slow but steady growth.[427] *The Listener* had 27,773 subscribers in its first year, and by 1935 the number almost doubled to 52,379.[428] While this total was admittedly small in comparison to the number of sets in the country, the publication fulfilled an important niche, provoked thought and undoubtedly launched several discussions amongst interested members of society.

The magazine's initial articles seemed apologetic that Britain had not embraced modernisms more enthusiastically. Despite society's long-term reticence, a new era had begun by the late 1920s, and although *The Listener* admitted that the changes in British architecture were "very wisely different from those of other countries" they were visible for all to see and to enjoy, including Celanese House in Hanover Square, Adelaide House at London Bridge and the Horticultural Hall in Westminster.[429] A June 1930 article by architect and author R. A. Duncan titled "The Architecture of the Future" admitted that if architecture served as a "barometer of civilization" then the nation was for changes "of the first magnitude". "Our tradition is breaking up", he confessed, "[and] old ideas can no longer control or point out with certainty the path for present day activities".[430] He interestingly predicted that architecture soon would reflect modern life to a greater extent than in the past because society was loosening its dependency on the individual and turning instead toward collective thought to solve complex problems of the day.

Photographic essays appeared regularly that highlighted the most modern British residential houses and public and commercial buildings while enthusiastically crediting the responsible architects.

---

427 Asa Briggs, *The Golden Age of Wireless, Vol. II* (Oxford: Oxford University Press, 1995), pp. 260-261.

428 Ibid.

429 Frederic Towndrow, "The Revolution in Architecture", *The Listener*, Vol. 1, No. 8, 6 March 1929, pp. 281-282.

430 R. A. Duncan, "The Architecture of the Future", *The Listener*, Vol. 3, No. 73, 4 June 1930, pp. 973-974; 1,000.

One essay depicted stunning images of ten structures including Thurso House (known today as Willow House), Cambridge by George Checkley; St. Church of St. Saviour, Eltham by the firm Welch, Cachemaille-Day and Lander; Freeman's Hospital, Ravenscourt Park by Sir John Burnet, Tait & Lorae; Royal Corinthian Yacht Club, Burnham-on-Crouch by Joseph Emberton; and "The Hopfield", St. Mary's Platt by Colin Lucas. Contained within this photo essay was a lengthy polemic titled, "Is Modern Architecture on the Right Track?", consisting of interviews with several well-known architects including Charles Holden, Wells Coates, Frederic Towndrow, Reginald Blomfield, M. H. Baillie Scott, E. Maxell Fry and Joseph Emberton.[431] Another photo essay highlighted the Daily Express building on Fleet Street and Hay's Wharf alongside the south bank of the Thames.[432]

In 1934 and in honour of the new Royal Institute of British Architects building on Portland Place, London, *The Listener* published a prescient article by Professor Charles Herbert Reilly, architect and head of the renowned Liverpool School of Architecture. He confessed that before the war, but certainly afterwards, the world was no longer content with looking backward to the past. While new ideas were being bandied about and experimented with by governments and architects, it was the young architects who were tackling contemporary issues with enthusiasm. "With them", Reilly argued, "the new problems of design are freed from its old conventions… " because the young and knowledgeable architects employed professional construction, heating, ventilation, sanitation, electrical and insulation engineers that were "extricating us from the complexities of modern life".[433]

---

431 "Is Modern Architecture on the Right Track?", *The Listener*, Vol. X, No. 237, 26 July 1933, pp. 123-132.

432 "The New Architecture in London", *The Listener*, Vol. VII, No. 165, 9 March 1932, p. 335.

433 Professor C. H. Reilly, "In Honour of the Formal Dedication of the New RIBA Building", *The Listener*, Vol. XII, No. 304, 7 November 1934, pp. 357-362.

The recognition of this new reality, Reilly argued, amounted to a revolution.

As the 1930s progressed *The Listener* expressed regular support for modernist architecture, continually praising its seemingly unambiguous, economical, efficient and unadorned simplicity. The rise of Nazi Germany and the general unsettlement throughout Europe caused the publication to refocus its priorities, thereby decreasing the quantity of articles that concerned modernisms. While *The Listener*'s influence remains open for debate, there should be little disagreement that the articles, the live broadcast transcripts and the photo essays certainly raised awareness and posited the belief, even to those not keenly interested, that modernisms no longer could be considered a temporary oddity. Britain understood it had to abandon the past as modernisms' innate dynamism assured its longevity within a changed world.

Modernisms made steady strides in the five years after the *Exposition des Arts Decoratifs et Industriels Modernes* exposed a cultural vulnerability. Britain probably would have accepted modernisms eventually but the Great War postponed by a decade any chance for a supportive following. The wrongful perception that modernisms were German-based coupled with general wartime xenophobia guaranteed that even the minutest progression would not be forthcoming. Victory assured many that Britain's powerful position in the world would remain unchanged from pre-1914 levels. Cynicism, disenchantment, disillusionment and despair dawned only in the late 1920s and early 1930s. As a "world leader", post-war Britain found little justification for embracing the "new" but the war had created an altered taxonomy of reality. And this, perhaps more than anything else, was what many found incredibly difficult to acknowledge.

The importance of this book is not to blame a reactionary society but to elucidate the concerns and issues surrounding the radical changes occurring in the cultural arts during the first quarter of the 20th century. The architecture and paintings designed and created in those years and the philosophies supporting them were dramatically different from anything that had existed previously. As amply demonstrated, the architectural profession's concern about the impact of modern art was legitimate. Modernist art influenced architecture. What once had offered aesthetic comfort, intellectual integrity and security suddenly seemed foreign and worrisome. The surety of hindsight enables us to feel a certain level of complacency and smugness: "There was nothing to worry about. Society simply overreacted. Change was inevitable so the public and the professionals should have got on and accepted it". To concede this as a legitimate response, however, is to ignore how genuinely troublesome and seemingly catastrophic these issues were for so many. In a time when society was experiencing several unsettling challenges – both real and imagined – from inside and outside the nation's borders, the last thing society anticipated was a total eruption within the cultural arts. Except for the protagonists, the majority of those who worked in each discipline believed the course had been determined long before and, despite minor alterations or subtle stylistic changes, would remain unaltered. The post-war era became a time of reflection, restoration and denial, allowing society to vent its spite toward long-cherished and traditional loyalties – patriotism, religion, morality and intellectual honesty. Those who thought life would continue as it had been prior to the war were unknowingly on the wrong side of history, unprepared to accept that the past lacked legitimacy. But the Great War had severed the present from the past forever. There could be no going back. By the late 1920s, British society and the architectural profession in particular recognized what it painfully did not want to concede: it had to go modern to remain viable.

Sources

Archival Facilities

Architectural Association School of Architecture, London
British Broadcasting Corporation, Reading, UK
British Library, London
National Archives of Great Britain, London
Royal Academy of Arts, London
Royal Institute of British Architects, London
Tate Britain, London
Victoria and Albert Museum, London

Periodicals/Journals

AA Notes
The Architect
The Architects' & Builders' Journal
The Architect & Contract Reporter
Architectural History: Journal of the Society of Architectural Histories of Great Britain
The Architectural Review
The Athenaeum
The Builder
Burlington Magazine
The Contemporary Review

The Egoist
English Review
The Journal of the Royal Institute of British Architects
The Listener
Nation
New Age
The New Freewoman
North American Review
Punch
Rhythm
The Studio
Week-end Review

Newspapers
The Daily Chronicle
Daily Express
Daily News
The Daily Telegraph
The Evening News
The Financial Times
The Morning Post
Pall Mall Gazette
The Times

Bibliography

Aldington, Richard. *Life for Life's Sake.* New York: The Viking Press, 1941.

Berghaus, Gunter, ed. *F.T. Marinetti-Critical Writings.* New York: Farrar, Straus and Giroux, 2006.

— — *International Yearbook of Futurism Studies Vol. 2.* Berlin: De Gruyter, 2012.

Berman, Marshall. *All That Is Solid Melts Into Air: The Experience of Modernity.* New York: Simon & Schuster, 1982.

Betjeman, John. *Ghastly Good Taste or a Depressing Story of the Rise and Fall of English Architecture.* London: Chapman & Hall, Ltd., 1933.

Blom, Philipp. *The Vertigo Years: Change and Culture in the West 1900-1914.* London: Weidenfeld & Nicolson, 2008.

Blomfield, Reginald. *Modernismus.* London: MacMillan & Co., 1934.

Booth, Allyson. *Postcards from the Trenches: Negotiating the Space between Modernism & the First World War.* New York: Oxford University Press, 1996.

Briggs, Asa. *The Birth of Broadcasting, Vol. 1.* Oxford: Oxford University Press, 1995.

— — *The Golden Age of Wireless, Vol. II.* Oxford: Oxford University Press, 1995.

British Art and Design 1900-1960. London: Victoria and Albert Museum, 1983.

Brooker, Peter. *Bohemia in London: The Social Scene of Early Modernism.* London: Palgrave Macmillan, 2004.

Bullen, J. B., ed. *Post-Impressionists in England: The Critical Reception.* London: Routledge Publishing, 1988.

Carr, Helen. *The Verse Revolutionaries: Ezra Pound, H. D. and The Imagists.* London: Jonathan Cape, 2009.

Carrington, Noel, ed. *Mark Gertler: Selected Letters.* London: Rupert Hart-Davis, Ltd., 1965.

Caws, Mary Ann and Wright, Sarah Bird. *Bloomsbury and France, Art and Friends.* New York: Oxford University Press, 2000.

Cork, Richard. *Art Beyond the Gallery In Early 20th Century England.* New Haven: Yale University Press, 1985.

– – *A Bitter Truth: Avant-Garde Art and the Great War.* New Haven: Yale University Press, 1994.

Crinson, Mark. *Modern Architecture and the End of Empire.* Aldershot, England: Ashgate Publishing, Ltd., 2003.

Curtis, William J. R. *Modern Architecture Since 1900.* London: Phaidon Press Limited, 1996.

Dannatt, Trevor. *Modern Architecture in Britain.* London: B.T. Batsford, Ltd., 1959.

Darling, Elizabeth. *Re-Forming Britain: Narratives of Modernity Before Reconstruction.* London: Routledge, 2007.

– – "Institutionalizing English Modernism 1924-33: From the Vers Group to MARS". *Architectural History* 55 (2012): 299-320.

Dean, David. *The Thirties: Recalling the English Architectural Scene.* London: Trefoil Books, 1983.

Edwards, Paul. *Wyndham Lewis, Painter and Writer.* New Haven: Yale University Press, 2000.

Eksteins, Modris. *Rites of Spring: The Great War and the Birth of the Modern Age.* Boston: Houghton Mifflin Company, 1989.

Eliel, Carol S. *L'Esprit Nouveau, Purism in Paris, 1918-1925.* Los Angeles: Los Angeles Museum of Art, 2001.

Everdell, William R. *The First Moderns: Profiles in the Origins of Twentieth-Century Thought.* Chicago: University of Chicago Press, 1997.

Exhibition of Works by the Italian Futurist Painter. London: Sackville Gallery, 1912.

Fahr-Becker, Gabriele. *Weiner Werkstatte, 1903-1932.* London: Taschen GmbH, 2008.

Farr, Dennis. *English Art, 1870-1940.* Oxford: Oxford University Press, 1978.

Fellows, Richard. *Sir Reginald Blomfield: An Edwardian Architect.* London: A. Zwemmer, Ltd., 1985.

– – *Edwardian Architecture: Style and Technology.* London: Lund Humphries Publisher, Ltd., 1995.

Fletcher, John Gould. *Life is My Song: The Autobiography of John Gould Fletcher.* New York: Farrar & Rinehart, 1937.

Ford, Boris, ed. *The Cambridge Guide to the Arts in Britain, Vol. 8, The Edwardian Age and the Inter-War Years.* Cambridge: Cambridge University Press, 1989.

Frampton, Kenneth. *The Evolution of 20th Century Architecture: A Synoptic Account.* New York: Springer, 2007.

Frantzen, Allen. *Bloody Good – Chivalry, Sacrifice, and the Great War.* Chicago: University of Chicago Press, 2004.

Frayn, Andrew. *Writing Disenchantment: British First World War Prose, 1914-1930.* Manchester: Manchester University Press, 2014.

Fry, Roger. *Catalogue of the Second Post-Impressionist Exhibition.* London: Grafton Galleries, 1912.

– – *Vision and Design.* London: Chatto & Windus, 1920.

Furedi, Frank. *First World War – Still No End in Sight.* London: Bloomsbury Publishing Plc, 2014.

Fussell, Paul. *The Great War and Modern Memory.* London: Oxford University Press, 1975.

Gay, Peter. *Art and Act on Causes in History – Manet, Gropius, Mondrian.* New York: Harper Row Publishers, 1976.

– – *Modernism: The Lure of Heresy From Baudelaire to Beckett and Beyond.* London: William Heinemann, 2007.

George, David Lloyd. *Speech Delivered by the Rt. Hon David Lloyd George, MP at the Queen's Hall London on September 19ᵗʰ, 1914.* London: Harrison and Sons, 1914.

Girouard, Mark. *Sweetness and Light: The 'Queen Anne Movement', 1860-1900.* Oxford: Oxford University Press, 1977.

Glancey, Jonathan. *New British Architecture.* London: Thames and Hudson, Ltd., 1990.

Glazebrook, Mark. *Unit One: Spirit of the 30's.* London: The Mayor Gallery, 1984.

Gold, John R. *The Experience of Modernism, Modern Architects and the Future City, 1928-1953.* London: E & FN Spoon, 1997.

Gould, Jeremy. *Modern Houses in Britain, 1919-1939.* London: Society of Architectural Historians of Great Britain, 1977.

Gradidge, Roderick. *DREAM HOUSES: The Edwardian Ideal.* London: Constable and Company, Ltd., 1980.

Graves, Robert and Hodge, Alan. *The Long Week-end: A Social History of Great Britain 1918-1939.* New York: W. W. Norton & Company, 1963.

Gregory, Adrian. *The Last Great War: British Society and the First World War.* Cambridge: Cambridge University Press, 2008.

Harris, Alexandra. *Romantic Moderns: English Writers, Artists and the Imagination from Virginia Woolf to John Piper.* London: Thames & Hudson, 2010.

Harrison, Charles. *English Art and Modernism 1900-1939.* Bloomington, Indiana: Indiana University Press, 1981.

Haycock, David B. *A Crisis of Brilliance: Five Young British Artists and the Great War.* London: Old Street Publishing, 2009.

Higgott, Andrew. *Mediating Modernism: Architectural Cultures in Britain.* Oxon: Routledge, 2007.

Hitchcock, Henry-Russell. *Painting Toward Architecture.* New York: Duell, Sloan and Pearce, 1948.

Hoffman, Alexander von, ed. *Form, Modernism and History: Essays in*

Honor of Edward F. Sekler. Cambridge: Harvard University Press, 1996.

Holroyd, Michael. *Augustus John: The New Biography.* London: Vintage, 1997.

– – *Lytton Strachey: A New Biography.* New York: Farrer, Straus & Giroux, 1994.

Hueffer, Ford Maddox. *Thus to Revisit.* New York: E.P. Dutton and Company, 1921.

Hynes, Samuel. *The Edwardian Turn of Mind.* Princeton, N.J.: Princeton University Press, 1968.

– – *A War Imagined: The First World War and English Culture.* New York: Atheneum, 1991.

Jerrold, Douglas. *Georgian Adventure: The Autobiography of Douglas Jerrold.* London: The 'Right' Book Club, 1938.

Kaplan, Wendy. *The Arts & Crafts Movement in Europe and America: Design for the Modern World.* London: Thames & Hudson, Ltd., 2004.

Karol, Eitan. *Charles Holden: Architect.* Lincolnshire, England: Shaun Tyas Publisher, 2007.

Kern, Stephen. *The Culture of Time & Space 1880-1918.* Cambridge: Harvard University Press, 2003.

Lane, Barbara Miller. *Architecture and Politics in Germany, 1918-1945.* Cambridge: Harvard University Press, 1968.

Lethaby, William R. *Form in Civilization: Collected Papers on Art and Labour.* London: Oxford University Press, 1957.

Lewis, Percy Wyndham. *Blasting and Bombardiering, An Autobiography 1914-1926.* London: John Calder, 1982.

– – *The Caliph's Design: Architects, Where is Your Vortex?* London: The Egoist, Ltd., 1919.

MacColl, D. S. *Confessions of a Keeper.* London: Alexander Maclehose & Co., 1931.

MacDougall, Sarah and Dickson, Rachel, ed. *Uproar! The First 50 Years of the London Group.* London: Lund Humphries, 2014.

Maciuika, John V. *Before the Bauhaus: Architecture, Politics and the*

German State, 1890-1920. New York: Columbia University Press, 2005.

Marwick, Arthur. *The Deluge: British Society and the First World War.* Boston: Little, Brown and Company, 1965.

Mayer, Arno. *The Persistence of the Old Regime: Europe to the Great War.* New York: Pantheon Books, 1981.

Mosse, George L. *Fallen Soldiers: Reshaping the Memory of the World Wars.* New York: Oxford University Press, Inc., 1990.

Muthesius, Hermann. *The English House, Vol. 1.* London: Frances Lincoln Ltd., 2007.

Nellist, John B. *British Architecture and Its Background.* London: MacMillan & Co., Ltd., 1967.

Nordau, Max. *Degeneration.* London: William Heinemann, 1895.

Nuttgens, Patrick. *Understanding Modern Architecture.* London: Unwin, Hyman, 1988.

Partnership in Style: Edgar Wood and J. Henry Sellers. Manchester: Manchester City Art Gallery, 1975.

Petherbridge, Deanna, ed. *Art for Architecture.* London: Her Majesty's Stationery Office, Department of the Environment, 1987.

Pevsner, Nikolaus. *Pioneers of the Modern Movement from William Morris to Walter Gropius.* London: Peguin Books, 1960.

Porter, Tom. *Archispeak: An Illustrated Guide to Architectural Terms.* London: Spon Press, 2004.

Pound, Ezra. *Gaudier-Brzeska, A Memoir.* London: Marvell Press Edition, 1960.

Powers, Alan. *Britain: Modern Architecture in History.* London: Reaktion Books, Ltd., 2007.

— — *Modern: The Modern Movement in Britain.* London: Merrell Publishers, 2005.

Rainey, Lawrence. "The Creation of the Avant-garde: F.T. Marinetti and Ezra Pound". *Modernism/Modernity* (September 1994): 195-219.

Read, Herbert, ed. *Unit 1: The Modern Movement in English*

Architecture, Painting and Sculpture. London: Cassell and Company, Ltd., 1934.

Reports on the Present Position and Tendencies of the Industrial Arts as Indicated at the International Exhibition of Modern Decorative and Industrial Arts, Paris, 1925. London: Department of Overseas Trade, 1927.

Reynolds, David. *The Long Shadow: The Great War and the Twentieth Century.* London: Simon & Schuster, 2013.

Rosen, Andrew. *Rise Up, Women! The Militant Campaign of the Women's Social and Political Union, 1903-1914.* London: Routledge, Kegan & Paul, 1974.

Rutter, Frank. *Art in My Time.* London: Rich & Cowan, 1933.

Sassoon, Siegfried. *The Weald of Youth.* London: Faber and Faber Limited, 1922.

Service, Alastair. *Edwardian Architecture and Its Origins.* London: The Architectural Press, 1975.

Schwartzman, Arnold. *London Art Deco.* London: Aurum Press, Ltd., 2006.

Sitwell, Osbert. *Great Morning.* London: The Reprint Society, 1949.

− − *Laughter in the Next Room.* London: The Reprint Society, 1949.

Skelton, Tim and Gliddon, Gerald. *Lutyens and the Great War.* London: Frances Lincoln, Ltd., 2008.

Smith, Bernard. *Modernism's History: A Study in Twentieth-century Art and Ideas.* New Haven: Yale University Press, 1998.

Stansky, Peter. *On or About December 1910: Early Bloomsbury and Its Intimate World.* Cambridge, Massachusetts: Harvard University Press, 1996.

Sutton, Denys, ed. *The Letters of Roger Fry, Vol. 1.* London: Chatto & Windus, 1972.

Tahara, Keiichi. *Art Nouveau Architecture.* London: Thames & Hudson, Ltd., 2000.

Tate, Trudi. *Modernism, History and the First World War.* Manchester: University of Manchester Press, 1998.

Thomson, David. *England in the Twentieth Century*. London: Jonathan Cape, 1964.

Thun-Hohenstein, Christoph, ed. *Ways to Modernism: Josef Hoffmann, Adolf Loos and Their Impact*. Vienna: MAK, 2014.

Tombs, Robert. *The English and Their History*. London: Allen Lane, 2014.

Tuchman, Barbara. *The Proud Tower, A Portrait of the World Before the War: 1890-1914*. New York: Macmillan Publishing Company, 1966.

Walsh, Michael J. K. *C. R. W. Nevinson: This Cult of Violence*. Cambridge: Lutterworth, 2008.

– – ed. *London, Modernism and 1914*. Cambridge: Cambridge University Press, 2010.

Watkins, Glenn. *Proof Through the Night: Music and the Great War*. Berkeley: University of California Press, 2003.

Weaver, Lawrence, ed. *Small Country Houses of Today*. Suffolk: Antique Collectors Club, Baron Publishing, 1983.

Wees, William. *Vorticism and the English Avant-garde*. Toronto: Toronto University Press, 1972.

West, Shearer. *Fin de Siecle, Art and Society in an Age of Uncertainty*. New York: The Overlook Press, 1994.

Weston, Richard. *Modernism*. London: Phaidon Press, Ltd., 1996.

Winter, Jay. *Sites of Memory, Sites of Mourning The Great War in European Cultural History*. Cambridge: University of Cambridge Press, 1995.

Wohl, Robert. *The Generation of 1914*. Cambridge: Harvard University Press, 1979.

Woodeson, John. *Mark Gertler: Biography of a Painter, 1891-1939*. London: Sidgwick & Jackson, 1972.

Woolf, Leonard. *Beginning Again: An Autobiography of the Years 1911-1918*. London: Hogarth Press, 1964.

Woolf, Virginia. *Roger Fry: A Biography*. Oxford: Blackwell, 1995.

– – *A Room of One's Own*. London: Penguin Group, 2000.

Yerbury, F. R. *Modern European Buildings*. London: Victor Gollancz, 1928.

Yorke, F. R. S. *The Modern House*. London: The Architectural Press, 1934.

Index